'Ivana powerfully exposes th[...] nation and online targeting [...] of AI, as a result, becoming our master not our servant. She also clearly outlines the radical changes to power structures and culture and the embedding of ethics which are necessary in finding the solution.'

TIM CLEMENT-JONES, Lib Dem spokesperson for
the digital economy in the House of Lords

'An essential read. At a time when we are fighting to put our environment at the top of the political agenda, Ivana Bartoletti lucidly demonstrates how another future for our digital environment is possible.'

METE COBAN, councillor for Stoke Newington
and CEO of My Life, My Say

'A powerful wake-up call. The link between AI, data and power can no longer be ignored, and, unless we take action, society's injustices will be written into all of our futures. Tech should benefit everyone and Bartoletti's book argues passionately for how it could and should improve our burning planet.'

AYESHA HAZARIKA, broadcaster and journalist

'Bartoletti demonstrates the potential for artificial intelligence to encode discrimination of all kinds into algorithmic patterns. Technology can improve our lives, but to harness all its positive potential, she rightly and powerfully insists on public accountability and scrutiny.'

DAVID LAMMY MP

'Bartoletti exhorts us at all times to bring our human intelligence to bear on the potentially dystopian power structures behind AI, writing with clarity, expertise and passion.'

PAUL MASON, author of *PostCapitalism: A Guide to Our Future*

'An absorbing and thought-provoking analysis of how technology is transforming our life, and a simple message: workers are far more than something for algorithms to hire or fire. AI holds promises and can make our life better but only if we, citizens, workers and trade unions are involved in the conversation.'

FRANCES O'GRADY, General Secretary of the TUC

'You can't enter the 20s without reading this book. It hurls a log into the path of the thunderous express train of technology. Bartoletti cuts through the hype of AI and gets to the nub of the problem: data violence. It's an angry book about the power politics of tech advancement where human rights and personal freedoms are mere collateral damage. Her feminist gaze is sharp on male technocrats using tech tools to manipulate and persuade politically. It is a tale of algorithmic injustice against women, ethnic minorities and people of colour. To say that it is thought-provoking would be an underestimate. I am still reeling from its power.'

NOEL SHARKEY, Emeritus Professor of Artificial Intelligence and Robotics at the University of Sheffield

AN ARTIFICIAL
REVOLUTION

ON POWER,
POLITICS AND AI

AN ARTIFICIAL REVOLUTION

ON POWER, POLITICS AND AI

IVANA BARTOLETTI

THE

INDIGO

PRESS

THE INDIGO PRESS

50 Albemarle Street
London W1S 4BD
www.theindigopress.com

The Indigo Press Publishing Limited Reg. No. 10995574
Registered Office: Wellesley House, Duke of Wellington Avenue
Royal Arsenal, London SE18 6SS

This edition first published in Great Britain in 2020 by The Indigo Press

Ivana Bartoletti asserts the moral right to be identified as the author of this
work in accordance with the Copyright, Designs and Patents Act 1988

First published in Great Britain in 2020 by The Indigo Press

A CIP catalogue record for this book is available from the British Library

ISBN: 978-1-911648-11-6
eBook ISBN: 978-1-911648-12-3

Design by www.salu.io
Author photo © *Global Woman Magazine*
Typeset in Goudy Old Style by Tetragon, London
Printed and bound in Great Britain by TJ International, Padstow

MIX
Paper from
responsible sources
FSC® C013056
www.fsc.org

To Ettore and Miranda,
and all the children of the world

CONTENTS

FOREWORD

This book draws on my experience as a feminist and as a data and privacy leader, and on my many years in politics, working with governments, corporations, international organizations, coders, and policymakers about data, privacy and artificial intelligence (AI).

I have concluded that technological solutions will not address the urgent challenges that AI and big data are bringing to our world.

As a feminist, I feel the need to challenge the myth of 'data neutrality' and to interrogate the gendered power dynamics that underpin the AI debate. Data is a form of capital, and it behaves as such, replicating the dynamics and inequalities of capitalism. Data collection is in itself an act of choice and, this book will argue, of violence.

As a privacy leader, I see the concept of privacy as a collective good being undermined. Our lives are being invaded by AI-driven algorithms, which increasingly drive our decisions, our desires and our political opinions. We are losing both our spontaneous human individuality and our sense of community as news and information become increasingly atomized experiences.

As a politician, I know that as AI systems are increasingly endowed with agency, and algorithms are progressively replacing policy-making, we will need to ask fundamental questions about what purpose this is serving.

Along the way, I will ask why we don't have an anti-AI movement like we have had an anti-nuclear movement. Without controls, oversight and international law, AI will be just as dangerous, and perhaps more so.

I must stress that this is not an anti-technology book – this is a book about technology and politics. I want people to understand that technology is not neutral. Technology is behind so much of the polarization and atomization of public life today, and technology itself won't fix this. Only politics will.

INTRODUCTION

Now is the time for a revolution: a revolution in how the forces that will shape our future will themselves be shaped. AI is political, and it is gendered.

The more women speak up and smash the boundaries in work, the more they are told that they are replaceable, as AI is allegedly coming after their jobs. Smart home technology is further enslaving women, and the more the #MeToo movement exposes how women are harassed at every corner, the more the market is inundated with subservient and flirtatious female personal assistants, ready – *programmed* – to be shouted at.

There is clearly an argument that this is the product of a resentful backlash from men claiming to feel displaced: the more progressivism brings freedom to women, the more AI products and services try to curb it – with AI ready to propel the male fightback. Within these pages I argue that this perceived male displacement is finding a voice in those new populisms around the world that are nurtured, fuelled and legitimized by AI-driven online manipulation. There is a direct and unmissable connection between AI and the political climate around the world, from Viktor Orbán to Donald Trump, by way of Jair Bolsonaro and Rodrigo Duterte. These populisms all have one thing in common. They advocate for a world where women are beneath men.

AI, automation and the digital ecosystem are at the heart of the problem, both as expressions of inequality and as the means to perpetuate it. Automation transforms the economy so that the kind of tax-and-spend policies that social democrats usually rely on become obsolete, making it incumbent on the left to rethink its approaches.

Populism also thrives on the digital ecosystem – and that is thanks in large part to the digital architecture of persuasion, control and oppression that has built up over recent decades. This architecture enables the collection, analysis and manipulation of our data to identify patterns of behaviour and to extrapolate our weaknesses, fears and desires.

The digital ecosystem is booming. Thousands of companies (some famous, some all but unknown) harvest our most intimate secrets, internet searches, online friendships and digital journey. They create profiles of individuals by hacking into our weaknesses.

All this is happening daily; the foundations of our democracies are starting to crumble, and we are not paying enough attention. With individual users having access to personalized news, we are losing the common shared knowledge that once bound us together as citizens. And what can we talk about if shared facts no longer exist?

It is as if we are all the subjects of some global conjuring trick, being distracted by the dazzling light of our shared digital future, and all we are supposed to do is marvel at AI's remarkable promise. The tech elites present us with a utopian future where AI solves all our problems, reads our minds, detects cancer more accurately and a decade earlier than any human doctor could, and is able to help us with our daily tasks.

Robotics technology will undergo rapid advancements, using artificial general intelligence (AGI), to the extent that some predict that robots will eventually be able to do pretty much anything humans can. But the simple fact is that, so far at least, AI artefacts can only do the tasks they are programmed to do, and nothing else.

While all this (alleged) progress happens, we are risking overlooking what AI can do right now: control, manipulate and remove our autonomy over our thoughts and choices.

In the global race to equip ourselves with the best technology, the trajectory of AI seems to mirror that of nuclear power. The more a nation embraces AI, the better equipped it is to compete internationally. We are in a new arms race, and this race has no end – indeed, no obvious goal in sight. This is a danger to all, not just in the future but in the present, especially when it happens alongside the rise of AI-fuelled populism, which is not merely arresting but reversing social progress along the way.

The power underpinning AI is data. Data, in its current form and scale, constitutes a new form of capital, and its extraction and exploitation lie at the heart of the rise of AI. Data is who we are; what constitutes our intimate being. It is our every online purchase, decision, opinion; every click of our keyboard; increasingly, every movement and sound we make in front of our computer is being turned into a commodity. The harvesting of us as data citizens through control, surveillance and constant monitoring is what makes data turn into capital and accumulation.

But data has a huge flaw, a flaw that is widely ignored or wilfully disguised: data is not neutral. It is inherently political. What to collect and what to disregard is an act of political choice. This means that every single AI artefact – be it a virtual personal assistant or a piece of software diagnosing the presence of polyps – is a political product. It is based on and extrapolated from existing data and therefore reflects the hierarchies and social structures we are immersed in. Data does not simply reflect society as it is, it also embeds those power structures into every corner of our lives by coding them into machines. These machines are increasingly 'softwaring' us out: they make decisions for us, shaping our lives and defining what we can and cannot see. They might determine whether we can be hired, whether we can secure a loan from a bank or receive government benefits, or if we should be placed on an at-risk register, with all that that might entail.

I must be clear from the outset: I am not anti-AI. AI has unparalleled potential to transform society for the better in any number of areas. But that AI has the potential to do good is not the point. Like nuclear power, AI can bring enormous opportunities but to do so, it requires a form of authority enshrined in global governance to avoid its terrifying downsides. Like nuclear power, we know that it will affect the politics and geopolitics of the world we live in. It will do so by reshaping labour, not just in terms of our professional lives but also in terms of the meaningfulness of life. These are profound and vitally important issues.

The recommendations of the European High-Level Expert Group on Artificial Intelligence include a suggestion that the focus should be on AI replacing menial jobs.[1] This may sound like a reasonable suggestion, but who defines 'menial'?

The crucial point I am making here is that AI is much more than technology. It is power, and, as such, it has power structures, and these can and do imply, even necessitate, dominance and oppression. All of this we are, perhaps naively, encoding into our systems. The implications are being felt and seen already; for instance in algorithmic racism and chauvinism: those pieces of recruitment software that will only recruit men, or the virtual assistants that, if harassed, will respond to the user with a submissive, coy flirtation,[2] instead of insisting that 'no means no'.

There is no simple solution. The fact that we can intervene in the products doesn't mean we can resolve the underlying problem. Fixing an algorithm will not answer the question of what, or who, AI is for in the first place.

It is not by chance that one of the tech mantras of this decade is that we need to get women into coding. Awards, programmes, mentoring and special events proliferate, but with little success, as women in AI are still less than 25 per cent of the workforce.[3] This is undoubtedly a challenge for our time, but it is only the start of the solution. Professional culture within the tech industry has to change – radically and quickly.

If AI is both power and oppression, we should claim the first, and resist the second. Resisting the second means understanding, not overlooking, what AI can do now. It means reclaiming our personal data, so we can stop the expropriation of our personal autonomy, choice and freedom of thought. There has to be true representation at all levels.

If AI is power, then it needs to be treated as such – and the battles are going to be on company boards, in government, in the media and in international institutions. That is where the law, the demand for accountability, funding and partnerships will be decided and shaped.

I

WHAT IS AI?

From driverless cars and smart homes to malevolent robots and unmanned military drone strikes… we are bombarded with images of what AI is supposed to look like. But what is this new age we are ushering in? What is this thing that we are told is going to take over the world, solve all our problems, recreate human life, run everything for us and eventually make us all jobless? We need to get it right, and to get it right we need to understand it. Definitions matter. To understand AI, we first need to understand intelligence.

The word 'intelligence' stems from the Latin *intelligentia*, which derives from *intelligere*, to understand. *Intelligere* is made up of two other words: *intus* (inside) and *legere* (to read). This is vital as it takes us straight to the point: *intelligentia* is the faculty belonging to whoever is *intelligens*, and the *intelligens* is one who can understand reality and the various hidden connections between the phenomena that constitute our experience.

Computer scientist Joanna Bryson asks, 'Is a thermostat intelligent, then?' It's an interesting question because a thermostat does indeed adapt and react to circumstances and realizes when it is time to turn itself on and off. So, to an extent, though a strictly limited one, a thermostat *is* intelligent. It regulates its behaviour according to the external environment. It makes a decision depending on the information it receives. Joanna's point is to show the limitations of this intelligence as she demonstrates that simply adapting does not fit the true definition of human intelligence.

We have generally understood human intelligence as the ability to accumulate and systematize knowledge, and to use it for higher cognitive functions. So, if human intelligence is about adapting to the circumstances in which we find ourselves, intelligent behaviour is the thing that identifies a course of action based on circumstances that may vary, radically and unpredictably.

Deep Blue, the chess-playing computer, did famously beat Garry Kasparov at chess, but Deep Blue didn't have Artificial General Intelligence and couldn't do activities outside its programmed capabilities, like food shopping. When humans can create artefacts (machines) that can do all the same things a human can do, only then will we be able to talk about AGI.

To put it simply, AI is (so far at least) about machines performing a task that humans perform and which is possible only because we, humans, have taught them to do so. The thing we program them to do is to recognize and act upon the correlation between things (*intelligere*); things that for us, humans, make up some part of what constitutes life and experience. Therefore, AI refers – to put it more technically – to artefacts used to detect contexts or to effect actions in response to detected contexts.

As a branch of computer science that focuses on the reasoning, perception and learning capabilities of machines, AI is not new at all. The word was coined in 1956 (although it was mainly known as 'Intelligent System' at that time). IBM played a key role in the 1960s, developing many new pieces of software and programs, which started to proliferate in academia and in many commercial applications.

However, while AI may not be entirely new, something has happened recently that has injected new enthusiasm into the dreams of researchers and corporations alike, and that is the development of so-called 'machine learning' (ML).

A central part of AI is ultimately about decision-making. In the context of AI, decision-making can be defined as analysing context and utilizing computational mathematical models to reach a decision.

Adding a learning element can significantly elevate the capabilities of an AI artefact, because it allows it to learn from its mistakes and adapt and improve its behaviour.

Automatic learning is perhaps the most exciting part of AI, as it means that a machine can learn to carry out a specific action even if that action has never been programmed as possible in the first place. To learn, a machine needs computational theory and analysis of patterns. Computation is what a computer does: it computes, which simply means that it makes calculations. It is important to demystify this word.

Patterns are trends that can be identified, informing a machine that there is a correlation between two things. For instance, if a machine is fed thousands of images of heart anomalies, it can learn what a heart anomaly looks like. The machine can then be used in a medical setting to spot cardiovascular anomalies present in patients. With the huge amount of data that we have at our disposal right now, machines could become exceptionally skilled at detecting anomalies – even those not visible to a human eye. And there is more: by looking at millions of images, a machine could identify the telltale symptoms that could diagnose a heart disease much earlier than we do now.

From cybersecurity to health, the potential of AI is startling, and most tech executives around the world would consider what I have just described to be the future of *all* industries, a glimpse of the glorious tech revolution about to come, or perhaps a revolution that we are living through already.

This revolution will include AI-driven classrooms where, from a very young age, students will have their learning programmes tailored to their capabilities. AI will be able to identify potential health issues before they develop and suggest ways we can prolong our lives. And if and when we reach old age, we will be looked after by automated care assistants. In fact, a wide range of AI products to support the elderly are already available: remote monitoring, voice assistants and even robots like ElliQ, branded as a 'sidekick for happier aging'. ElliQ can talk, remind older patients to take their drugs and encourage them to keep active.[4]

However utopian the vision of the near future that the tech elites present, the reality is likely to be very different. Machine learning is a labour-intensive activity. Training a machine requires a vast number of workers, who are often underpaid and unrecognized.

It is hard to see a starker contrast than that between the highly paid male execs in Silicon Valley, where the median pay for a top 100 CEO is $15.7 million a year,[5] and the quotidian reality of women in India who are feeding endless images of polyps to the information-hungry machines on which they labour. Cade Metz, writing for the *New York Times*, captured the settings in which this type of intensive labour takes place,

The offices could have been call centers or payment processing centers. One was a timeworn former apartment building in the middle of a low-income residential neighbourhood in western Kolkata that teemed with pedestrians, auto rickshaws and street vendors.[6]

What happens in these centres is closer to traditional factory work than the futuristic fantasies that the tech world are selling. For a few pennies per label, workers identify the telltale signs to teach a machine what a disease looks like. Metz reports of a female worker who would, over the course of a typical eight-hour day, watch about a dozen colonoscopy videos, constantly stopping and rewinding the video to look more closely at individual frames. On finding evidence of a polyp, she would 'lasso' it with a 'digital "bounding box"', repeating this process hundreds of times over the course of the day.[7]

Similarly, many tech workers across the world spend their working days going through violent images to teach a machine what abusive imagery looks like so it can be removed from the internet. This is an unsettling and anxiety-inducing job, with known and unknown psychological consequences for those engaged in it, as employees have reported post-traumatic stress disorder, chronic insomnia and a generalized, debilitating fear.[8] Imagine having to watch scenes of child abuse for hours on end every single day. This is the reality of the technological revolution towards which we are being marched. This is the reality that lies behind Facebook's claim that they are using tech to remove pornography and extremism from their platform. They are using tech – but behind that tech is a lot of exploitative and degrading human labour.

This is not some troublesome outlier in the otherwise pristine, clinical world of tech. A substantial proportion of the spend on AI is on this hidden cost of labour.[9] Far from the perceived glamour of Silicon Valley, or the tech fairs showcasing the shiniest of all worlds, for now, ML requires a lot of cheap human labour. Contrary to the promise of the millions of desirable jobs that AI will inevitably create, this technology is producing a lot of invisible, demanding, low-paid jobs in poorer areas of the world.[10] Although we can't overlook the fact that, for some, this unenviable work is a ticket out of poverty (and perhaps the only one).

Another consideration is important for our understanding of these processes: that the learning can be supervised or unsupervised. In supervised learning, a coder gives the machine the relationship between an input and an output – and then the result. The coder then asks the machine what the general rule is that makes it happen so that every time a single input is given, it will choose the correct output.

The process of learning can be unsupervised, too. This is when the machine does not have a 'teacher' or a coder giving the machine inputs – it simply learns by itself. This is particularly relevant to 'clustering', which is when a machine is asked to find correlations that are not visible to the human eye. It is like asking an algorithm to cluster people you have met at a party without giving the machine any characteristic or indication of what to look for. This is an extremely powerful resource, as a machine can identify patterns invisible to human perception.

ML is progressing rapidly, thanks to the vast amount of data available to study (and learn from), which has propelled progress in AI and ML over recent decades. The fact that we collect data all the time and everywhere (especially because of the abundance and diffusion of cheap interconnected technology in general, and smartphones in particular) means that there is a proliferation of data available out there for AI to benefit from.

Data-collection points are in operation at every step of our daily lives. Information about where we are, our journeys to and from work and what we are listening to is collected in our connected cars and public transport. Data about how many people live in our house, if we are home or not and if we use a kettle or another product can be inferred from our smart meters' use. We have become a form of data, and data has become a buzzword – something we hear about all the time as a sacred resource that allows us not only to understand what is happening around us but also to interpret, decide and drive choices. The term is 'data-driven': a new mantra of our times.

The word 'algorithm' derives from the twelfth-century Persian scholar al-Khwarizmi (then Algoritmi in Latin) and was used to define the step-by-step performance of elementary arithmetic. An algorithm is generally viewed as a series of defined steps undertaken to produce particular results. A coder will write those steps using one of the languages available on that specific machine.

An algorithm looks and functions somewhat like a mathematical formula: a set of instructions expressed in code. In practice, an algorithm is a mathematical construct that makes a decision based on these instructions and on the information that is given as an input.

This is how AI works. When we produce a machine, we produce an artefact that makes decisions, identifies anomalies and performs specific tasks. These artefacts could be anything from a piece of state apparatus, such as a system to identify which families may be at risk of poverty, to more complex artefacts such as robots, those human-like objects that behave like us, and can even shed a tear. Humanizing robots is very much a trait of our time, and, indeed, programming them to shed a tear or two is part of this project. This is a contentious matter because by humanizing them we are, in reality, giving them some agency which is, at the present time, a huge leap into the unknown.

I often ask people how they feel about AI, and their responses are, inevitably, informed by science fiction. Every single time, someone brings up robots and super-intelligent machines that can turn against us, in the manner of *The Terminator*, *The Matrix* and other visions of a machine-controlled future.

We are far, far away from that, from robots and machines that behave like us – from a so-called AGI. For now, this is a fantasy. The difference between AI and AGI is simple. AI artefacts can perform the task they are set to perform. AGI artefacts can, hypothetically, do what we do. So, for example, an AI artefact will probably be able to identify laundry baskets and sort clothes by colour but will not be able to decide what items are for dry cleaning only. AGI is what the techno-elites around the world are after, and that is the replication of human life.

It seems possible, perhaps even probable, that as technology evolves, robots will inhabit our world, challenging the concepts of sentience and consciousness as we know them. But sentient robots don't yet exist outside of science fiction, and it is critical for us to recognize the technological age we are living in right now.

Our obsession with the imminent arrival of super-intelligent robots is by no means confined to the media, to newspapers and film producers latching on to big, attention-grabbing ideas to drive the sales of whatever it is they are peddling. Recently, at a UN conference on education, a delegate from a small, resource-rich but (as is sadly often the case) cash-poor country told me that soon AI will replace politics and politicians. He was understandably worried by this fanciful vision of the near future, and I was troubled about his anxiety. This man's concern may be justified, but its focus is misplaced. The focus on robots, general intelligence and a terminator is a big distraction, a way to keep most of us in if not blissful then at least useful ignorance, preventing us from asking the key questions: who and what is AI for?

While the marketing departments of big corporations or well-funded AI start-ups continue to feed us with the wonderful promises of tech lying ahead of us, we should all be thinking – and worrying – much more about what AI can do now. We are repeating the same mistakes that we made with the internet. The internet has allowed us to explore new possibilities and to feel more connected than ever before. With it, though, the infrastructure that has been created has changed our privacy, the way we live and the control we have over our information.

The law was far behind from the start and has been struggling to catch up ever since. We have used the internet as a space to imagine and create – in many ways good things – without limits and without rules. This explains the distortions and the dangers of our current digital space. Legally, politically and ethically, we are still playing catch-up.

The problem now is that we hardly know what we should be worrying about. From time to time, socially conscious tech workers who want to do the right thing by building tech for expressly good purposes have given us glimpses into the bleak reality of, say, facial-recognition products by putting themselves in the firing line, by risking their livelihood, even their own personal safety, for the future of us all. For example, hundreds of Google employees launched a petition for an assurance that the company will not bid on a government cloud-computing contract that could be used to enforce US immigration policies on the southern border.[11]

The limited ability we have to hold the architects of this technology to account is owed to these brave people – not by default, and not through any existing legally, politically or ethically based supervision.

That is deeply troubling, and fraught with danger, because AI is reshaping the world right now, with us having little say on it.

We are told that any form of enforced accountability would stifle innovation, harm our economic future and delay inventions which could change our lives for the better. The faster we move on from this false and threatening dichotomy, the better it will be for all our futures.

2

CHALLENGING THE SANCTITY OF DATA

We can think of an algorithm as a machine with an established function or series of functions. Once an algorithm has the data and some parameters to relate the data to and classify it, it can be set to make decisions and to learn how to make better ones. For example, if a business decides to use an algorithm to choose the best-qualified individual for a job, it may wish to set some guidelines for what a good employee looks like and let the algorithm identify the prime candidates.

This applies to other sectors. With all the data we now have, we can train machines to learn to make decisions and to perform whatever task they are set to perform clinically, objectively, and without prejudice or bias.

Data is collected every moment of our life: through our smartphones, when we touch our cards on public transport, through all the connected devices we use and during our browsing on the web. Recent estimates suggest that humanity generates around 2.5 quintillion bytes of data every day[12] – enough, if printed, to create a pile of paper that would stretch nearly one and a quarter times around the earth.[13]

Let's take the example of a fridge. Until recently, a fridge was a pretty simple analogue device: a tool to store food and keep it cold. Some have now become 'smart', which means they monitor what we buy, like and consume. That data can then be used for marketing, to send us specific products and recipes and to monitor our eating habits. There are, almost invariably, unforeseen consequences of technological evolution, and recently a smart fridge was used by a teenager to tweet, as her parents had confiscated her mobile phone.[14]

The collection and analysis of this huge quantity of data is possible because of the increased computing power we now have, which is only going to increase still further with the 5G network coming into our lives.

Before we look at the politics of AI, it is necessary to understand the politics of data. I want to challenge the basic idea that data can inform better decisions because of the inherent integrity within it. The concept is that as data mirrors society, and reflects it honestly, then the data must be 'true', and the AI applied to it will be able to read it and so drive our policies.

A delegate of a national education system at an international meeting recently told me there was 'no need for judgement, just use data!' This concept is what I call the 'sanctity of data', and it is a dangerous one, especially for women and the most vulnerable in our society.

Data is not neutral, and the fact that we collect a huge amount of it brings many challenges – not just from the standpoint of privacy but also from the standpoint of power dynamics.

What we must never forget is that data is not simply information. It is our public and private desires, our likes on Facebook, every purchase made, and every opinion expressed. These are all expressions of ourselves: our identities, our personalities. Data is, essentially, what constitutes us as human beings, and it should be treated as such.

I first became interested in data because I was alarmed at the proliferation of CCTV cameras in the United States, where I was studying as an exchange student in 1996. I remember feeling oppressed by the sense of being watched at all times, but even then it was more than that. It felt more like being invaded.

This commodification of our personalities into raw material is what underpins the data economy, which drives the collection of information during every moment of our daily experience. We have blindly accepted that we are being studied and analysed to train machines, our behaviours becoming fuel for algorithms so they can serve us the adverts they think we will buy into, that our consumption of energy at home, which represents the way we live our life, is being analysed, allegedly to offer us the best service.

We have internalized the idea that there is nothing more objective, more neutral, more informative and more efficient than data. This is misleading. When an algorithm is fed data, a decision has already been made. Someone has already decided that some data should be chosen, and other data should not. And if data is, in reality, *people*, then some of us are being selected while others are being silenced.

We can see this play out in the medical field. Medical research analysing what causes strokes has progressed rapidly over the past few decades, but it was only very recently that it emerged that the symptoms of heart diseases in women are different from those in men, which has led to very serious consequences in terms of prevention and detection of illness for half the population. Why did this happen so late? Simple: because, until then, most of the research was focused on men and used men's bodies and data. Another example is endometriosis. As reported by Huntington and Gilmour in 2005,

The time period between initially seeking medical help to a diagnosis being made typically took 5–10 years... Characteristically, diagnosis was a time of relief [...] after years of having experiences negated by medical authorities and being told the pain was a normal part of menstruation. Women's feelings that their pain was being dismissed as imaginary have also been noted in other studies.[15]

Endometriosis is common. About 10 per cent of women suffer from it. And yet, according to Morassutto et al. (2016), it's quite possible that about six out of ten cases still go undiagnosed.[16] In reality, women know that pretty much any pathology that disproportionately affects them follows similar patterns: misdiagnosis, lack of understanding, dismissal, mistreatments.

To understand why this is happening, we need to look at the non-neutrality of data: medical research is still a male-dominated field, where men overwhelmingly decide what to study and what not to study, thus informing which data is collected and which data is excluded.[17]

Choosing data to train algorithms means making a choice about which individuals will form the data set, the consequences of which can be profound and pervasive. Any sense of objectivity here is wholly illusory. Think about surveys. To collect data around victims of a particular crime, we would get a far more accurate (and higher) figure by asking victims anonymously than by asking local police forces to report the figures voluntarily. This is because a lot of crime doesn't get reported – especially around domestic abuse. And what is reported may not give the true picture of crime occurrences in one area – this can cause problems if data is uncritically used to inform and decide the allocation of resources. And consider how the allocation of resources and policy decisions might shape how a local authority would respond to and support women suffering from domestic abuse.

The choice about which data sets are studied is being made by people. It is a subjective decision, and a political one. Each individual, once entered into a data set, becomes part of a new transaction between them and the unseen force that has put them into it, and has used that data set to train an algorithm and ultimately make a decision about them.

This represents an asymmetry of power, and this asymmetry – the outcome of choice and power – is what underpins the politics of data and, ultimately, the data economy. The data economy is political at every level, not least because some organizations hold a huge amount of power over others by deciding who gets onto a data set, and who is left out, a decision that may have far-reaching implications.

I often talk about data violence, and that is because I see an intrinsic violence in choosing or disregarding data. It is a new form of violence, a new way of silencing people – and an insidious one; not only because it is more subtle and less understood than others, but because it is uncontested.

British activist and journalist Caroline Criado-Perez, in her book *Invisible Women*, shows the sometimes fatal consequences of ignoring or excluding data about women, from healthcare to industrial design to urban planning.[18] Her examples are deeply shocking, and range from Siri, who could give you information about Viagra, but wouldn't know where to find the nearest abortion clinic, to the way we have designed our cities to serve the mythical male breadwinner with a home, wife and kids in the suburbs.

Choices about data are a matter of power, and this power dynamic needs to be interrogated because it lies at the very heart of the model of our data-driven society. We have already seen how diseases mostly affecting women have been less studied than others, with much less data available about them. If we look again at how algorithms work, we can take this argument to a greater and graver level.

Algorithms need to be fed data, but because data, and the choices around it, reflect current societal structures, the output of the algorithm is likely to be the product of those same societal structures. With algorithms now being used for everything from determining access to loans to deciding who to release from jail, who should receive an immigration visa, who to hire and who should be assigned social housing, this issue is becoming ever more important.

And, indeed, a lot of literature has been produced recently under the heading of algorithmic bias: namely that, as algorithmic predictions are built on historic data, which means past decisions made by humans (and therefore incomplete and, as we have seen, representing and mirroring structural dynamics in our society), their output is likely to be biased too.

At a recent AI conference in London, I heard Evanna Hu, CEO of tech company Omelas, describing three types of bias.

The first she called 'pre-existing bias', and that is bias that emerges straight out of existing data. That is what happened in 2016, when researchers at Google unleashed a neural network on a corpus of 3 million words taken from Google News texts. The neural net's goal was to look for patterns in the way words appear next to each other. This product was called Word2vec, and it was powerful. For example, if you typed 'France: Paris as Japan: x' the system would return the word 'Tokyo'.

But the product was also remarkably chauvinistic. So if you asked the database 'father: doctor as: mother: x' it would say 'x = nurse'. And the query 'man: computer programmer as: woman: x' gave 'x = homemaker'. The reason was that the data came from the internet and the historic data it contained.

The second type of bias Hu defined as 'technical bias', something that Virginia Eubanks, Associate Professor of Political Science at the University of Albany, discusses in her book, *Automating Inequality: How High-Tech Tools Profile, Police, and Punish the Poor*. She gives the example of the Pennsylvania child triage system, a statistical model supposedly able to predict which children might in the future be victims of abuse or neglect. Predictive models use statistics to predict which parents might maltreat their children.[19] But the data serving as their foundation was collected only on families that use public programs, leading to hi-tech risk detection systems that confuse parenting while poor with poor parenting.[20]

The third kind of bias Hu called 'emerging bias', something that happened with Microsoft Tay. TayTweets was an account controlled by AI, designed to learn from conversations on social media. What happened, though, is that Tay soon started to put out highly offensive content, including, 'I fucking hate feminists and they should all die and burn in hell.'[21] Tay was the victim of a coordinated attack with lots of people tweeting awful things at it, and that is where it learned its language. What is disappointing, however, is that no one had taught Tay's developers and publishers – or taught the system – about this potential outcome and how the system could have learned from the environment in which it was set to operate.

Bias is complex and mostly inevitable. An AI arte-fact will be fed data, which is data that somehow or other represents the world as it is now. But that is not the only reason. An artefact is the product of who has decided to put it together and decided what to use it for. As such, bias is always present. What I also find troubling is the idea that a technical fix can resolve such problems.[22] Many readers will have heard of Amazon having to pull out of the release of a piece of recruitment software when it emerged that it would only pick up male CVs.[23] Using AI, specifically ML, the tool in question reviewed job applicants' résumés and assigned each of them a score from one to five stars. To produce its ranking, this AI was trained by spotting patterns in résumés submitted to the company over the previous decade. However, given the under-representation of women in the technology industry, the vast majority of these résumés belonged to male candidates.

Inevitably, based upon this data, the AI system learned to favour males. So, for example, if a résumé included the word 'women's' (for example, 'women's chess-club captain'), or the names of all-women's col-leges, then the system would disregard it. Instead, it would favour lexicon like 'executed' and 'captured', commonly found in male engineers' self-descriptions.

This applies to images as well as words. In 2018, Google announced that it had fixed its Photos applica-tion, which was mistakenly identifying black people as gorillas. The application uses ML to recognize people, places and events depicted in photographs and to automatically group those with similar content. Three years after Jacky Alciné, an African-American consumer and developer, pointed out that Google Photos labelled photographs of his friends and him with the tag 'gorillas', all that the company has managed to fix was completely removing the tag so that the ML algorithm does not assign it to any image whatsoever.[24]

We have seen how some of the bias is due to technical factors: AI needs data, and data reflects the bias in society. The problem lies with characterizing this structural discrimination as bias. As algorithms are increasingly deployed by our local authorities, banks, hiring companies and the health sector to make decisions and to perform tasks on our behalf, the issue of outputs reflecting structural inequality and power imbalances in society will be escalated to a new level – and this is happening with little or no scrutiny.

Women have fought for centuries to make organizations accountable for discrimination, and now we are finding all this returning through the back door of automation. By calling this 'bias', we are making two dangerous mistakes. Firstly, we are humanizing these machines by attributing to them human characteristics, and, by doing so, we are shifting the responsibility away from us to the artefact. AI is a human tool, created, developed, organized and fed data by humans. When

AI goes wrong, we are both the victims and the perpetrators. The responsibility is ours and absolving us from the outcomes of algorithmic decisions is a grave error.

Secondly, by calling it 'bias' we are missing the real issue. It is not simply bias. If it discriminates on the grounds of race, it is racist. I am struck by how reluctant we are to say 'algorithmic racism' or 'algorithmic chauvinism'. Instead, we revert to the use of the soft term 'bias'. Are we really supposed to accept that, because humans can be racist, it is by extension somehow acceptable for unaccountable, uncontrolled and proprietary software to embed that racism into every corner of decision-making, so it becomes ingrained and, worse yet, unchallenged?

Let's take the issue of housing. Alongside education, housing is one of the biggest opportunities for people to get out of poverty. So what happens when algorithms make decisions about assigning homes to families? It is an interesting question because the answer is, remarkably, unknown. It is not by chance that in the United States a new housing and urban development department is discussing proposals that would give landlords much greater protection from discriminatory claims.[25] The reality is that most of the products that government agencies use come straight off the shelf: they are pieces of proprietary software covered by commercial interest, thus making the system unaccountable. And even if accountability tools were introduced, the reasons underpinning discrimination can emerge at different stages of the process.

Let's say the police want to identify who is more likely to carry a knife. In this case they would look at statistics related to who has been found carrying a knife in a particular time frame to identify patterns of behaviour or common characteristics. But, again, it is easy to imagine how skewed that data set is likely to be: we know that black people are more likely to be stopped and searched by the police.[26]

The increased use of these algorithms for decision-making or for making predictions means that algo-sexism and algo-racism are reaching a completely new level, unaccountable and unchallenged, embedded in the very fabric of our techno-chauvinistic societies, which means that we are being fed by public-relations departments, as well as austerity-inclined politicians, the message that tech is, necessarily, better, cheaper and more efficient.

The shrinking of public-sector services often means that local authorities and agencies are receptive to the idea of saving money through automated systems with the alluring prospect of efficiency and cost-cutting. Why employ a human to decide who to assign a house to if an algorithm can do it? And why not use ML to analyse patterns, thus identifying which families are more at risk of poverty, payment arrears or gambling addiction?

The problem, though, is that these analyses inform policy decisions and the allocation of resources. If the data ingested into the system to determine these decisions has the power-related complexities we discussed above, the outcome will be that both the patterns and the solutions informed by them will reinforce society as it is now, rather than breaking the cultural and social norms underpinning it and thus transforming it for the better.

Perhaps the biggest misconception about AI is that, because humans are biased, irrational and emotional, we must automatically welcome algorithms as they are by nature 'scientific', thus not deformed by cultural norms. Or, even, that we can code 'fairness' into those algorithms by virtue of a mathematical fix.

This simplistic view does not take into account the power relation, discussed already, between who is in a data set and who has decided to put them in it. If society as it is today is the only model we use to train algorithms that are going to affect us tomorrow, then we risk hard-coding injustices and prejudices into societies of the future.

To solve this problem, we must change the vocabulary around it, first by eradicating the word 'bias', which is an easy way out for companies who can – or can at least claim to – offer a technical solution to it. Instead, it is time we acknowledge that data is simply not neutral, and, as such, every single decision and action around data is a political one. How we respond to algo-sexism and algo-racism is through politics, not through algorithmic fixes.

The obsession with fixing algorithms is a smoke-screen, and, for some, a rather useful one because it deters us from acknowledging the real issue, and that is the power dynamics underpinning algorithms and, therefore, the entire data economy.

In 2018, Sundar Pichai, the CEO of Google, told a town-hall event in San Francisco that AI is one of the most important things humanity is working on: 'It is more profound than, I don't know, electricity or fire.'[27] That sounds bold, but it is arguably true, and to fully appreciate his claim we need to look further into what underpins AI: namely, data.

Some insist that data is the new oil, and that is an interesting and illuminating comparison, though a limited one – firstly, and most obviously, because data can be used over and over again. Unlike oil, it is not a finite resource. And secondly, and more importantly, it is a limited comparison because I think it is time to start seeing data not as a commodity but as capital.

The reasons for this are, in my view, clear. For example, companies like Siemens or GE now present themselves as data firms rather than technology companies.[28] Data has been the driver and the underlying reason for many acquisitions, including Amazon's purchase of Whole Foods for $13.7 billion in 2017.[29]

There is little doubt that the accumulation of data is a core component of the political economy in the twenty-first century.[30] We need only consider the power of Facebook and Google, the vast amount of data they have amassed and are continuing to amass about us, as well as their power over politics and regulators alike. Some will recall Facebook CEO and founder Mark Zuckerberg being questioned by (mostly clueless) US Congress members about what Facebook does and doesn't do – what its business model is and how it operates.[31] This was a clear example of the chasm between tech and politics, with politicians simply not grasping the extent of the digital realm and its influence on the world we inhabit.

If data accumulation is a core component of the political economy, 'data extractivism' is the tool behind it. Extracting data is the way to grow power and influence. And because data is capital, it behaves like capital. At a global level, data is becoming a geopolitical arsenal that is creating a new form of colonialism, whereby large corporations take over the digital infrastructure of the Global South for exploitation and control. For example, Netflix is increasingly buying up a lot of content from Africa[32] and now ranks at number one in the generation of internet traffic at a global level.[33] Meanwhile, Uber's aggressive expansion into the taxi industry in South Africa led to escalating violence during 2017's 'Uber wars'.[34]

Similarly, China has signed an agreement with Zimbabwe to deploy facial-recognition software, developed by CloudWalk Technology, which will prove invaluable for China as the country needs non-Asian faces to train its algorithms for facial recognition.[35] Another example is UK-based firm De La Rue rolling out the ID programme in Rwanda, collecting the biometric data of all citizens.[36]

In recent years, one tech company in particular has generated headlines, and that is Jumia, known as 'the Amazon of Africa'. Jumia operates in fourteen African countries and is the first Africa-focused e-commerce company to be listed on the New York Stock Exchange. Customers can order anything from an iPhone to a chicken korma at the touch of a screen.

The success of Jumia is particularly interesting and revealing, considering that many African countries have put their faith in 'leapfrogging' – the idea that developing nations in Africa can skip whole stages of development. Jumia does indeed fit that narrative and gives many Africans hope for a future in which e-commerce, not extraction, becomes the engine of African growth. Cities like Lagos boast vibrant tech districts, and more and more people are using apps.

However, critics have started to question how well Jumia is serving the denizens of Africa. Jumia was in fact incorporated in 2012 in Berlin, though it has been known to tell inquirers that it was headquartered in

Nigeria. It was originally called Kasuwa, which means 'market' in Hausa, a language used in northern Nigeria. Later, it was renamed Jumia. At the most senior level, the company is managed not by Africans but by French executives, who were operating out of Paris until they moved to their current headquarters in Dubai. Much of Jumia's capital was raised in Europe and America.[37]

People started to wonder how different Jumia was from companies like Shell, a large corporation that employs lots of Africans but can hardly claim to be African. Rebecca Enonchong, a Cameroon-born tech entrepreneur living between Africa and the United States, sees Jumia as a foreign company dressed in African robes. Jumia, she says, is the brainchild of Rocket Internet, a German company that 'copy pastes' ideas developed in Silicon Valley and applies them to the rest of the world. 'This is a Rocket Internet company. It is not an African start-up. We have a painful history with European companies, this colonial legacy that is very recent. It seems like it's being repeated in the start-up world.'[38]

These examples and the debates they generate go to the heart of what many refer to as 'digital colonialism'. The issue is not whether companies from all over the world should be trading in African countries. It is, rather, that African institutions are outgrowing their local ecosystem, as it is very difficult to match the cash injections Western companies can provide.

My point, though, is that this taking over of the digital infrastructures could lead to a real form of extra-territorial jurisdiction, and that is the main danger in my understanding of data as capital. The question, therefore, becomes whether or not the accumulation of data will increase the global divide, exacerbating the dramatic consequences that we all see unfolding around us already, from forced migration to the threats to our environment.

3

ALGORITHMS AND
THE RISE OF POPULISM

As human labour is increasingly replaced by machines making decisions and performing tasks on our behalf, it is no surprise that – as they are fed data – algorithms have the power to embed those global and local power structures in every element of decision-making they now govern. And, make no mistake, they govern more and more of our lives.

Scientists tell us that AI technologies are still in their infancy. If you need an insight into the limitations of AI today, read the account of the very unautomated automated car journey described by Meredith Broussard in her brilliant *Artificial Unintelligence: How Computers Misunderstand the World*.[39] However, my fear is not what AI will be able to do at a certain point in the future. I am optimistic about AI-driven advancements in sexual reproduction, medicine and disease detection. My fear is, as outlined earlier, the acute, rational anxiety in the face of elements of what AI can do right now. This is already a serious problem and it may well prove to be disastrous – especially for women.

The most disturbing application of AI right now is online manipulation, 'the use of information technology to covertly influence another person's decision-making'.[40] This is possible because AI allows political influence to move from public campaigns to the manipulation of our private sentiments, thanks to supercomputers (complex, interconnected algorithms), pointed at us all the time as we navigate our way through the digital world.

Feminist-hating populism is being fuelled by online manipulation, which is happening across the world from Trump to Salvini, from Boris Johnson to Viktor Orbán. Populist parties and politicians use digital tools to override traditional media, which they perceive as biased against them. And by doing so they have been able to inundate the digital world with messages that are less visible in traditional media. The issue is that the vigour of populism at this present time cannot and must not be analysed without taking into consideration how new technologies and AI-driven advertising enable these movements to thrive by reshaping the political agenda. All of this is possible because of how the digital infrastructure works, because of the business model of social media companies and the inherent inequalities of data sets. All of us, and women in particular, should fear the AI-driven digital advertising ecosystem, which is bringing back arguments, language and visions of the world that we fought so hard and for so long to get rid of.

In June 2019, President of Russia Vladimir Putin said that liberalism is 'obsolete',[41] the implicit argument being that human rights, privacy and individual autonomy are incompatible with the tech-dominated economies in which we live. This is not just Putin's argument. I often hear at industry conferences around the world that it is impossible to thrive globally in the digital race we are in if we want to safeguard individual rights and privacy the way we do now.

In other words, human rights and personal freedom are collateral damage in the ongoing battle for technological advancement. The argument goes like this: ML and AI are the future because they will enable economies to run faster, productivity to increase, and all sectors to thrive. For this to happen, though, businesses, nation-states and academic institutions alike need access to data, and that is not possible if restrictions are placed on the sharing of information, or if we need individuals to consent to their information being broadcast to the myriad organizations that may wish to use them. The General Data Protection Regulation in the European Union, which came into force in May 2018, was seen by some as stifling productivity as it was introducing too many restrictions in how data is handled.[42]

That is the argument in brief. From time to time, prominent business analysts get on stage to claim that we face a choice between, on the one hand, innovation, allowing the trickling down of wealth, and, on the other, privacy and restrictions to the broadcasting of personal data. China, business analysts argue, is able to develop AI at such a fast rate because its government has access to data without limitations. The same may well apply to the United States, although things are changing amid various scandals – the misuse of data by Facebook, Google, Amazon et al.[43]

I struggle with this argument. With the danger in sight, and some of it already in full display, I am not sure we have agreed what the endgame is. Nor can I understand the urgency or the desire to rush towards a future that, instead of unleashing the potential of technology, will see our rights curbed by it. If the end point we are striving for is authoritarian surveillance capitalism or new wide-ranging forms of control over our every movement, then I am happy to slow things down, to call for a pause and the chance for reflection about where we are going, and whether it is worth it.

And a pause is perhaps what we need most right now. In 2018, the Western world gained a little more clarity about what the unethical use of tech looks like. The company Cambridge Analytica illegally harvested the data of 57 million citizens and allegedly played a key part in the campaign to leave the European Union, as reporters like Carole Cadwalladr revealed in the pages of the *Guardian* and the *Observer*.[44] It emerged that Cambridge Analytica obtained data from Facebook as users had their data exposed through Facebook's quiz app. That data was then allegedly used for microtargeting and behavioural advertising to users without them knowing. Cadwalladr and others predicted much of the situation we are in now, and that is because they saw first-hand the power of big-data analytics, of AI-driven online advertising and how those tools can be used by the powerful forces driving a populist agenda.

In 1840, Henry David Thoreau described how the tranquillity of his home, near Walden Pond in rural Massachusetts, was interrupted by visitors leaving traces of their passing through:

> When I return to my house, I find that visitors have been there and left their cards, either a bunch of flowers, or a wreath of evergreen, or a name in pencil on a yellow walnut leaf or a chip. They who come rarely to the woods take some little piece of the forest into their hands to play with by the way, which they leave, either intentionally or accidentally. One has peeled a willow wand, woven it into a ring, and dropped it on my table. I could always

tell if visitors had called in my absence, either by the bended twigs or grass, or the print of their shoes, and generally of what sex or age or quality they were by some slight trace left, as a flower dropped, or a bunch of grass plucked and thrown away, even as far off as the railroad, half a mile distant, or by the lingering odor of a cigar or pipe. Nay, I was frequently notified of the passage of a traveller along the highway sixty rods off by the scent of his pipe.[45]

It is interesting to think about the traces of ourselves we would have left behind before the digital age: a scent, footprints, some object or other. Our lives now are very different, and the collection of our digital footprints is what is driving the success of hundreds of companies, large and small, in the online ecosystem.

Web-browsing provides a goldmine of information, as what we do says a lot about us: what we like and don't like, who we hang out with and how wealthy we are. Data extraction – squeezing out every possible facet of our personality by analysing how we behave, which websites we visit and where we travel – is a lucrative business and defines and drives how news and products are advertised to us.

Wendy Hui Kyong Chun suggests that network analytics can be read as 'the bastard child of psychoanalysis'.[46] What Chun means is that our disparate activities online make us surveilled citizens. The outcome is that our relationships, our responses to news and announcements, and the ideas and emotions we express online are analysed to create profiles: a synthetic personality to be targeted, predicted and advertised to.

Online advertising is what we see when we navigate the web. It is the pop-up that follows us from one site to another. It is the order in which news is presented to us. And it is the post on Facebook we see first when we log in. It also defines what we can and cannot see. Traditionally, there are two kinds of online advertising. One is contextual: if you are looking at shoes, an advert about shoes will appear. The other is behavioural, and the role that AI plays in this form of advertising is quite disturbing.

Tristan Harris from the Center for Humane Technology describes this brilliantly: algorithms are creating a race to the bottom of the brain stem, to extract attention by hacking lower into our base instincts – into dopamine, fear, outrage.[47] That is, in essence, what behavioural advertising is: it is made by powerful algorithms hacking into our emotions, fears and desires; hacking into our humanity to extract patterns so that they can decide what to sell us.

If, for example, a company wants to sell shoes, they can rely on insights provided by our behaviour. If the shoes are fashionable, they can look for people who are of a certain age, character and background, who live in certain postcodes and who earn a certain amount of money. This is possible because our information is broadcast on the internet. The Facebook business model, for example, is not to sell user data but to provide sophisticated analytics and tools to advertisers so they can target us with what they want.

As I write, over 2.4 billion people use Facebook and over 2 billion use YouTube.[48] The power of these social media platforms is vast, insidious and dangerous. As long as it is about shoes, it may not seem particularly worrying. But what happens if our personal traits and choices are used to form profiles to drive us towards more significant decisions?

Netflix created thirteen profiles of individuals to promote *House of Cards* to. For each profile, it identified a particular angle to spin so as to catch interest. That could range from targeting particular people with a particular scene, to highlighting black characters for black people.[49]

These techniques are complex and can be used for films or shoes... or politics. One thing I find especially alarming is that many of the best and brightest minds of my generation have been wasting time mastering learning how to place ads online, to win this race to the bottom of the brain stem. Instead, they could have been focused on how to solve the real, pressing problems of our world, starting with climate change.

What developers have now created is something rather terrifying: they have made machines so powerful, so intrusive, so capable – while we are still all too human. Whereas machines may, in some ways, know us better than our partners or parents, and these algorithms can predict what we like, don't like or might like in the future, we are still essentially the same humans we were thousands of years ago. Our capacity hasn't really evolved; our feelings are not that much different from those of our prehistoric ancestors. We still feel the same basic fear, love, jealousy, desire and rage that we felt at the beginning of human history. Machines, meanwhile, have evolved rapidly in a matter of decades. They can now outperform us in human and post-human tasks – and I am not talking about robots or AGI (which is, as discussed earlier, AI that is able to do things it wasn't programmed to do). I am talking about algorithms capable of understanding if we are gay before we know it, if we are entering a manic stage before we become aware of this ourselves, or if we are pregnant.[50]

Looking into this, one wonders how it happened. How could we have allowed a system to grow by extracting our weaknesses, rather than our strengths? Whether they are selling us shoes or an anti-immigration message, these algorithms pinpoint, target and exploit our intimate secrets, sensitive information and vulnerabilities. Machines know how to keep us engaged – if we are losing interest, they pick up on that and find a way to re-engage us. Savvy marketeers know how to put content in front of their users. Their algorithms can measure when someone's interest is decreasing so that a more suitable ad can be served. Our weak points are churned through algorithms and extrapolated for the big shares of big tech.

Our addiction to our online life is also affecting the way we inhabit our physical and emotional lives. Younger generations struggle with detachment, bring their devices into their bedrooms and are unable to switch off from the messaging, the targeting and, all too often, the hatred directed against them. Our attention span is now limited, and the inability to focus for prolonged periods of time is a new, widespread human trait.[51] The continuous flow of information means we can only consume subheadings and are unable to cope with the complexity and nuances of comprehensive investigation. Whenever I tackle this issue, I come across an obstacle: the alleged realism people put in front of me. Here's the most common example, 'Everyone uses social media, it's so useful!' And, indeed, it is, to an extent. One has to acknowledge the benefits of our connected, digital world. Social media has enabled some people to find justice.

A filmmaker I met in China told me that she broadcast the story of a Tibetan woman who faced horrendous gender discrimination in her family of origin in Tibet. After moving to Beijing with her child, this woman faced racism and violence on the streets of the capital city. She was discriminated against twice: as a woman in Tibet, and as a Tibetan in Beijing. Her son is now in an American school and is doing well.

'This wouldn't have been possible without Facebook', the filmmaker told me in response to a disparaging remark I made about Mark Zuckerberg. What she was explaining was that, because the story was published on the social media platform, and liked by thousands of people, it was also picked up by the media in the US and a school ended up offering him a place. They both moved there. That is undoubtedly true, and there are other stories along these lines, but is that enough? Is it enough for Facebook to act as the saviour for a few individuals while being also used to spread propaganda by the Myanmar military for over half a decade?[52]

We must ask what the long-term effects of containing and conveying acts of kindness, affection and social responsibility within market-led models will be. Will we still be able to mobilize people to campaign for justice and take action if and when the goals of these campaigns do not fit the logic of the market in which they happen?

The fact remains that their business model is perverse: Facebook makes money by keeping us engaged so that our data can be extrapolated, so that the platform can be used by advertisers to target us based on the granular information Facebook has about us. The good news is that tech industry workers seem to be increasingly aware of these issues: a recent Doteveryone report shows that tech workers are increasingly socially conscious with nearly two thirds reporting that they would like more time and resources to think about the social impact of their products.[53] There is hope, after all.

We should not blame big tech alone – that would be too simplistic. We took far too long to develop privacy legislation, and it is hard to blame companies for exploiting that vacuum, making money out of it and improving their technologies in the process. We are where we are: only now, AI-driven online targeting is taking advertising to a completely new level. This needs sorting out before we lose the autonomy to think and to shape our own lives.

As I write, regulators and legislators are grappling with all this, and certain companies are making changes – largely cosmetic ones – to their practices. Google, for example, has announced some limitations to its broadcasting of data in the digital ecosystem.[54] However, without complete systemic change these steps will not be enough.

I got into privacy from a human rights standpoint when I was working as an adviser to the Italian Human Rights Minister, Barbara Pollastrini, in 2007. However, as we were trying to push a progressive agenda, the dangers of data and the digital infrastructure to push a conservative agenda became apparent to me. I became interested in ideas of privacy while I was witnessing the erosion of personal autonomy, which in my view privacy is about: a great collective good, rather than a selfishly individual one. Privacy, as I have seen and studied it, has not caught up with the world as it is now. And I'd go further still and say that if we do not change our approach to privacy, we are not going to get people on board in the attempt to take ownership of the future of AI and algorithms.

Privacy is conceived of as an individual right. For example, the campaign in the UK against the 2006 Identity Cards Act, which, if enacted, would have created national identity cards linked to a database, showed the depth of opposition to the infringement of people's privacy. I often wonder why there isn't the same outrage around algorithms, face recognition and online surveillance? It seems possible that people are happy to lose some privacy in return for something they value as consumers. Privacy in the identity card campaign was viewed as an intrusion into their rights as citizens, while online tracking and micro-targeting relates to their identity as consumers and are therefore not perceived as serious infringements.

Privacy is a culturally constructed concept; it changes depending on the time and place. In China, for example, citizens' behaviour is monitored to ensure it is in line with state expectations and is rewarded with better treatment when accessing services. In France, on the other hand, information about race cannot be asked for at recruitment stage. Privacy changes with technology, too, as we adapt to the benefits of being connected. Those who have tried to stay off our connected technologies know how difficult it can be. But there is something disturbing about the discrepancy between what we hold dear as citizens and what we are giving up as consumers, especially as our new identity as data citizens blurs the distinction between consumers and (traditional) citizens.

I think it is now time to redefine privacy around freedom from persuasion, even freedom from being nudged towards a particular choice. In a digital age, we should be able to claim the right to our own journey through life without the intrusion of algorithms. It is about dignity. The persuasion architecture that underpins the world of social media is a breach of our essential rights as human beings, our integrity, our true selves.

The constant monitoring of our feelings through algorithmic extrapolation is happening with far too little input from citizens, and in the process we are being discreetly deprived of our humanity. As we edge towards the artificial, this is troubling and must be addressed before the artefacts we create take us even further away from choice and autonomy.

One positive emerging from the debates around AI is that we will be forced to reflect, more than ever before, about what it means to be human. And if being human means to feel truly, then is persuasion not the exact opposite?

What I am talking about is the reconfiguration of privacy as the right to navigate our way through life without facial expressions being scrutinized in a shop for companies to be able to serve us what they think we like or need or want the most. Or the right to change our opinion and not to be steered into a specific retirement scheme because we fit a pattern of people who have chosen that scheme before.

If we redefine the concept of privacy around persuasion and the right to personal freedom of choice, the asymmetry of power between big tech and us, the people, becomes ever clearer. This is an essential step in taking ownership of our future.

One problem with the architecture of persuasion is that it benefits populists around the world. The messages they propagate can be fuelled online and served to exactly the right people thanks to the obscurity and complexity of algorithmic-driven advertising.

Philosophy professor Luciano Floridi talks of how marketing has extended to politics.[55] Politics is changing, becoming ever more focused on leaders and less on content and nuance. This is true – and it is terrible news for women. Berlusconi, Bolsonaro, Duterte, Farage, Johnson, Salvini and many other populists are, Floridi says, the result of the marketization of politics – and the marketization has coincided with the extraction and manufacturing of personal data thanks to algorithmic-driven software.

The polarization of public discourse has seen a new convergence between populism and data-manufacturing, with the ability to harness and exploit people's fears with populist messages. Women are the victims of all this. Take the conservative politicians in the United States who claim that abortion is to blame for illegal immigration. Their argument is that the 'number of women getting abortions since its legalization has decreased the labor supply, and therefore undocumented persons are encouraged to cross borders illegally to fill the demand for labor in the US market'.[56] The link between being anti-choice and anti-immigration emerges from time to time but, through the internet, it has found a new way to reach exactly those more likely to buy into this narrative.

Let us look for a moment at the degradation of public discourse in relation to women's bodies and women's dignity. Take Donald Trump and the language around him and used by him. Outside rallies, Trump supporters sell T-shirts saying, 'Don't be a pussy, vote for Trump'. Meanwhile, crowds shouted, 'Lock her up!' in reference to his rival presidential candidate Hillary Clinton. And who can forget Trump calling his rivals 'ugly', or saying that women let him 'grab 'em by the pussy'? Bolsonaro's approach is not vastly different.

Both talk about the return of a glorious past. This is always a warning sign, as the glorious past usually means one where men were in charge. Like Trump, Bolsonaro rose to his position by attacking a woman, Dilma Rousseff (a woman who had been the victim of torture at the hands of Brazil's military rulers). Bolsonaro's infamous comment to a Brazilian congresswoman – 'I would never rape you, because you do not deserve it'[57] – has a chilling effect on women, and on all decent people, worldwide.

In the 2019 UK general election campaign, Boris Johnson stubbornly refused to apologize for saying that women in burkas 'look like letter boxes', even though it is well documented that Islamophobic attacks increased significantly in the aftermath of his remarks. This is the world we live in. Duterte in the Philippines is another example. Although he did not have a female predecessor or rival to destroy, he worked on fears, focusing on drugs and promising to restore law and order. In 2017, Duterte "joked" that because he had declared martial law on the island of Mindanao, soldiers could each rape three women with impunity.[58] In 2018, he told soldiers to shoot female rebels 'in the vagina' because that would render them 'useless'.[59]

Dehumanizing, insulting and undermining powerful women – indeed, all women – is a trait across all populisms. It is not my intention to blame social media for the rise of populism, but it is my intention to show that it has been perhaps the most effective tool of populists. Because, alongside stagnating incomes for many and the steady increase in inequalities on a global scale, the politics of hate and the use of AI-driven behavioural advertising and predictive technologies cannot and must not be ignored. Without challenging the proliferation of hate online, of fake news and disinformation, women will see old attitudes resurfacing, and this is a threat we must confront.

Women's bodies are one of the biggest political battlegrounds of our time. Partly, it is, as it always has been, because what should be personal – a woman's body – is made public and political. Alabama has enacted some of the most egregious legislation regarding reproductive rights, denying choice even in the case of rape or incest.[60] This is not an isolated example. Around the world, most populist leaders advocate for the return to an era where women were consigned to the domestic realm, with little if any control over their sexual lives and fertility. The role of AI-driven advertising within this must not be underestimated: 63 per cent of the top links related to abortion news on Facebook came from right-leaning sources, and many of the most widely shared links referenced debunked or misleading narratives about abortion, like the idea that Democratic politicians are endorsing 'infanticide' by supporting abortion access later in pregnancy.[61]

The reality is that our values are also being eroded. Each and every one of us is receiving personalized advertising and personalized news, served to us based on our synthetic personality. News is becoming personal, leading to the disappearance of a shared, common base of knowledge upon which democratic debate is built. This is happening against a backdrop of growing populism, the rise of misogynies old and new, and the erosion of democratic values and rights. Democratic viability requires the ability, the obligation, to discuss what is a shared truth around facts – but does that still exist?

We must change the language around bias, and so we must change the language around personalization, as it is precisely this language that allows politics to move from an overt to a covert script, thanks to online behavioural and predictive tools. These predictive-analytics tools are pieces of business-intelligence software that can help predict actions: for example, they can be used to pinpoint segments of a population that are more likely to buy a product or engage with a campaign.

Personalization, profiling optimization, customization – these are all buzzwords of marketing and PR, helping to euphemistically present individual marketing as a bespoke experience, rather than the exploitation of our vulnerabilities, passions and fears for the benefits of corporations and political groups. There is nothing personal in this process: the personalization of our online life is the exact opposite of nurturing our uniqueness. It is, effectively, the shutting down of democratic debate and autonomous thought for the benefit of the shadowy big data operations run by the billionaires supporting populisms worldwide.

There is one statistic, in particular, that should give us pause: while Netflix created thirteen profiles for personalized targeting of their product to their customers, the Canadian company AggregateIQ, commissioned by the Vote Leave campaign in the UK Brexit referendum, created 1,433 customized adverts combining a Brexit message with one that tapped into the longings and anxieties of Facebook users.[62]

Harvesting the data was only one part of the company's plan. What we saw in the 2019 Netflix documentary *The Great Hack* was that Cambridge Analytica tried to manipulate emotions and target people based on their fears and psychological vulnerabilities, hacking them when they felt worthless. AggregateIQ and Cambridge Analytica are connected. There is a service agreement and an intellectual property agreement between AIQ and SCL (which is the parent company of Cambridge Analytica). This is the true scale of the persuasion machine, and it is operating on a global scale.[63]

4

AI AS CONTROL

It has often been said in recent years that the process of data extraction through constant surveillance is a major driver of capitalism as we know it today. This phenomenon has been described in different ways: surveillance capitalism, communicative capitalism, platform capitalism, or iCapitalism.

To describe the world around us as being comprised of 'data' is an inherently political statement, as, in doing so, we commodify the objects, experiences and connections we encounter in our daily lives. We have become accustomed to this data imperative, to the extent that we no longer challenge it, implicitly justifying its existence and legitimizing the power that the data firms have over us.

Writer Jathan Sadowski expresses it beautifully, 'to know the world is to exercise power over it, and to exercise power is to control it – to examine its features and characteristics, to sort it into categories and norms, to render it legible and observable'.[64] To categorize and extract therefore means to exercise power, and that is why everything that we do and are incentivized to do has become a way of producing data.

We are incentivized to drive automated cars so we can produce data, and to use connected devices like smart meters so we can generate more information. Cars, smart meters and the like are therefore no longer just commodities, objects and more or less useful things. They are tools allowing companies to market us, segment us, surveil and manipulate us.

This is happening all around the world. In early June 2019, young protesters took to the streets of Hong Kong to oppose a proposed extradition bill that would have allowed criminal suspects to be sent to mainland China to face trial. The protesters were demanding that their governor safeguard the rights that the citizens of the peninsula were promised and to protect them from the threat of direct Chinese rule.

One morning, as the protesters were travelling to the main square for another demonstration, something happened: they hesitated at the subway's electronic gates and chose to use cash to purchase their tickets instead.[65] In other words, they decided to dodge China's digital surveillance machine while the government was ramping up its use of technology to control and surveil civilians.

Everyone who has been to China has felt that strange sensation of having their face scanned or, at the very least, of knowing their face was being scanned, at every corner. The feeling is an odd one: at first, it changes the way you inhabit public space, turning you into a cornered animal, looking around continually, determined to show you have nothing to hide. After a while, though, being watched becomes normalized.

The society of surveillance works like that. Data-collection points pick up information about the way we drive, the way we walk, the shops we visit, the lifestyle we lead. If a citizen behaves well, the Chinese Social Credit System rewards them with lower insurance premiums or easier access to housing. That is the deal: persuasive, seductive authoritarianism.

Networked technologies are often seen as a tool to galvanize support, but they can turn into enemies of the freedom to protest by tracking activists on social media as well as following the digital trails we leave behind us, including when we take public transport or when our face is scanned and matched against millions of other faces.

In the aftermath of the Arab Spring, the enthusiasm regarding the capacity of Twitter and other social media to support the protesters soon vanished. In the beginning, social media's role was transformative, and the attempts of the regime to respond were counterproductive. Zeynep Tufekci describes how 'Egypt's weary autocrat, Hosni

Mubarak, had clumsily cut off internet and cellular service. The move backfired.'[66] In fact, what happened as a result was that the flow of information coming out of Tahrir Square did stop, but this caused an immediate and dramatic increase in the international focus on Egypt. Within a few weeks, Mubarak was forced out.

What happened next was scarcely less remarkable. Those in power learned from Mubarak's mistake. Egypt's Supreme Council of the Armed Forces opened a Facebook page, and, as one supporter put it, from this point onwards, 'the online sphere became full of bickering between dissidents who were being harassed by government supporters'. Digital technologies went from being a beacon of democracy, able to offer a space and voice for dissent, to becoming tools of oppression and discord.

It would be a mistake just to point the finger at China or other authoritarian countries, to single them out as the only examples of surveillance and intrusion. It is a global phenomenon. The West has its own version, in what academic and writer Shoshana Zuboff describes as 'surveillance capitalism', where the data collected about us is 'fed into advanced manufacturing processes known as "machine intelligence" and fabricated into *prediction products* that anticipate what you will do now, soon, and later'.[67]

Segmentation, profiling and the surveillance of citizens have always happened, but, with the use of algorithms, the automation of manipulation has taken on a completely different dimension.

Facial-recognition techniques are a clear example of this. The capacity to match your face against millions of others stored in the databases of governments and private organizations alike is perhaps the most obvious and disturbing expression of this new power. Facebook uses it when it suggests the names of people as we upload photos onto our profiles, and Amazon has developed a piece of software, Rekognition, which is sold to police agencies in the United States, despite concerns among the employees and the tech workers who have developed the product itself.[68] As a whistle-blower put it, 'Companies like Amazon should not be in the business of facilitating authoritarian surveillance.'[69]

There are problems with this software, too, especially, as discussed already, in relation to their inability to properly recognize black faces, thus discriminating by erroneously finding positive matches. Most of the scary stories about facial recognition in relation to ethnicity come from the United States, which could be because, historically, not only are the US data sets more skewed towards black, Asian and minority ethnic citizens, but also because there has been more attention paid to this and more investigative journalism carried out in the United States than elsewhere.

Facial-recognition techniques, which automate existing inequalities and racism in society, are used with little oversight and control. However, outrage and pushback are happening already: San Francisco was the first US city to ban them, in 2019.[70] Coincidentally, those who profit from the sale of surveillance technology are also the ones who get to escape its dangerous effects.

As I write, during the aftermath of more mass shootings in the United States in August 2019, and as people mourn the loss of their loved ones, a new proposal has emerged, and it is not the obvious one of simply curbing the sale of guns.

The *Washington Post* reports that the White House has been briefed on a plan to create an agency called HARPA with the aim, among other things, to monitor 'neuro-behavioural' predictors of violence.[71] This rather dystopian idea involves collecting data from smart devices, including Apple Watches, Fitbits, Amazon Echoes and Google Homes, with the purpose of identifying the signs of someone headed towards a violent, explosive act. The project would use AI to create a 'sensor suite' to flag mental changes that make violence more likely. This is, to say the least, alarming and is yet another tool of social control under the dystopian banner of predicting the unpredictable.

If there is one common element in all the mass shootings we have seen around the world, it is that the perpetrator tends to be male and often a man with a history of overlooked domestic abuse towards women.[72] Why isn't this unambiguous fact looked at rather than trying to identify some (non-existent) correlation between how much someone walks and their likelihood to commit an attack?

Not only is this dangerously short-sighted, wrong-headed and an insult to women, but also, by putting so much emphasis on an alleged relationship between mental health and violence, it further marginalizes those with mental health issues who might think twice before asking for help out of fear of being put on a federal watch programme.

Furthermore, what happens if people do end up on such a watch list? Would it, for instance, make it more difficult to access housing or a loan?

In a different sector, take Pennsylvania's Allegheny Family Screening Tool (AFST), a decision-support system used to predict child abuse or neglect at the time of birth and to alert social services to children who may be at risk. The attention of child services can have profound effects on the lives of families whose risk score is high. Contact with social services is one factor that may lead to a higher predictive score, so some families feel they must engage in self-harming behaviour, withdrawing from 'networks that provide services, support, and community' to optimize their score. AFST might 'create the very abuse it seeks to prevent'.[73] This is a clear example of what Virginia Eubanks defines as a new digital poor-house, which is using data collection to wrap around and control segments of population more tightly.[74]

Ultimately, these privacy-stripping practices lead to all this data being aggregated and analysed through predictive algorithms, which are used to craft the policies and rules that then apply to people's lives, and the lives of their children.

In *Weapons of Math Destruction: How Big Data Increases Inequality and Threatens Democracy*, Cathy O'Neil argues that algorithms are mathematical models that can sift through data to locate people who are likely to face great challenges, and she poses the key question of whether this form of control is there to punish or to help.[75] Right now, AI is getting a bad reputation as most of the applications seem to be around the former, and perhaps it is time to move to the latter if we are to restore trust in the digital world.

5

RESHAPING LABOUR

The accepted attitude in recent years has been that if you are critical of AI and concerned about what is happening to the labour market, you are, without question, anti-technology, anti-modernity, anti-innovation and anti-progress. But if AI is actually going to replace human tasks, we need to have an honest and open debate about it, one that does not shy away from uncomfortable avenues of thought.

Firstly, some human tasks are better off being performed by machines. Why would we want to engage in mindlessly repetitive activities when these could be performed by machines instead? Or in dangerous, life-threatening ones? The question should be about governance, how we can plan the future ahead, and, ultimately, how we can drive the direction of AI development in a structured way.

Secondly, we are concerned – and rightly so – about jobs disappearing, because, for millions, the only alternative to a job is destitution. To understand the impact of AI on labour, we need to look into two main areas: firstly, how AI is reshaping the concept of labour; and secondly, how different the era we are in is from previous automation revolutions.

AI is creating new forms of modern unpaid labour, of which people need to be made more widely informed. In sharing all our information on social media platforms, we labour for them. This is not just a semantic curiosity. It is a fact. This is what we do when we go through all the trouble of posting pictures and crafting articulate, intricate messages about our thoughts and ideas on social media.

We give social media companies all they need to train and improve their algorithms, and we do this for free. Their business model is to make us work without pay. We upload photos so they can train their facial-recognition software. We react and comment on our friends' posts so they can produce the best prediction software to hack into our personalities. We spend money online so our consumer habits can be identified, encoded and extrapolated, allowing advertisers to target us with products to spend more money on. This is a new form of unpaid labour, and we seem to be unaware of it. We do it because their systems are good; they satisfy us; they entertain us.

Let's take the example of companies operating in the healthcare sector. Access to data means that the potential for research improves dramatically. However, we should be asking what the public healthcare of a nation gets in return for making all its data available? If a pharmaceutical company uses the data to produce a groundbreaking new drug that has the potential to save millions of lives, the company is going to sell it to the same healthcare system (and many others too) for distribution. But how will they pay back the organization that gave them the raw material that enabled them to produce the drug in the first place?

I would question the fact that national healthcare systems are not getting anything in return – nor are individuals. This is worrying for us all, and health is not the only territory where this is taking place. Take Uber, which is changing the way we move around our cities. Uber is making transport cheap by undercutting salaries and pressuring drivers into achieving unreasonable targets. Sophisticated algorithms present drivers with arbitrary targets at the very moment they are about to log out and stop working.[75] This is to pressure them into continuing to drive.

What happens, though, if exhausted drivers fall asleep at the wheel and end up in road accidents, putting their safety and the safety of everyone else at risk? So far, no law has been able to challenge Uber's practices, although the Mayors of London, Sadiq Khan, and New

York, Bill De Blasio, have shown real teeth in ensuring technology is accountable and safe for citizens.

It seems like governments have to become arbitrators between AI-driven solutions and older institutions that many feel are at risk of obsolescence; for example, the threat to the hotel industry and associated job losses posed by Airbnb.[76] The problem runs deeper than that as big data and algorithmic solutions threaten to replace the labour of policymakers themselves.

Mosaic is a service run by Experian, and their offering is to enrich data with publicly available information, to provide local authorities with predictive information about the areas they govern. While I don't underestimate the importance of big data in producing useful insights, I object to politics and political choices being replaced by algorithms. What happens, for example, if data shows that wealthy people live in a particular area, and that spots of poverty are located in others? Public policy would inevitably allocate resources in a certain way. The problem is that political choices would then be deprived of what, in my view, is their essential function – to *transform* – and by basing their decision on algorithms they would perpetuate inequalities and stereotypes. Tech thrives, while funding for public services is reduced.

The deception here is that an uncritically pro-AI movement continues to highlight how new technology will bring new jobs, but ignores how tech is changing the nature of work itself. For many people, labour is the single most important thing they rely on for a sense of identity, and AI is threatening not only jobs but also the very essence of labour, which has for centuries dominated the political landscape. With data as capital, labour is changing, and this has dramatic consequences that require new politics.

AI and the training of algorithms is not just fancy open-plan offices in Menlo Park, California or trendy working spaces in Shoreditch, London. There is another face of AI. It is much more sinister, and it's something we have touched on already. It's the tens of thousands of people employed at $28,000 a year by third-party contractors to vet millions of appalling images and videos to check whether they can remain online;[77] people who develop post-traumatic stress disorder, insomnia and panic attacks owing to the constant exposure to hate speech, violent pornography, cruelty and sometimes murder of both animals and humans for Facebook, YouTube and other media platforms.[78] While the average annual salary at Facebook is $240,000 in the USA,[79] these underpaid, unacknowledged workers are part of the secret AI workforce that no one wants to talk about.

Google employs over 100,000 people, as reported in the *Guardian*, in what one company employee called a 'white-collar sweatshop' workforce, to create the hand-crafted data sets required for Google Translate to learn dozens of languages.[80] There is a huge disparity between these workers and the full-time Google employees living in the hippest, most desirable places in the world.

Mary Gray and Siddharth Suri call this AI global human supply chain 'ghost workers'.[81] And ghosts they certainly are, especially as hardly any mention of them has ever been made during the countless AI ethics symposiums I have attended over the past few years.

So, my great concern is how AI is accelerating not just the loss of jobs but the impoverishment of labour. And that is not only because, by scrolling and posting on social media websites, we labour for free for the benefit of the big companies using our data but also because of the hidden workforce in AI, the ghost workers described above.

And there is more. Algorithms that can learn bring a different approach to automation itself. In part, it is true that automation is not a new thing, as of course we can see with the industrial revolution and countless other technological advances. But with ML, there is a dramatic difference. With ML, developers build a model that learns by itself. More specifically, the model learns a solution to a problem, while before labour was all about learning a solution from someone else who had that specific knowledge.

To understand this, let's consider spam filters: they learn that an email is unwanted and put it into the spam folder. They continue to do so with our input, and, progressively, they get it right more often. AI is about classic automation – a machine learning from a human – as it was with the previous industrial revolution. But algorithms that learn by themselves bring an unprecedented dimension to the concept of labour: they learn to learn.

We could go as far as to say that ML is more than automation – it is the automation of automation. And this is not without far-reaching consequences. Workers using ML can automate their own work. In the evolution of labour over the centuries, a crucial factor has been its increasing detachment from capital. The culmination of that was reached with the financialization of the economy, when labour was finally split from the immaterial wealth of the financial services, a shift that has been taking place gradually throughout the post-war period. This has brought into starker relief the disparity between earnings from your own labour, and capital gains from the immaterial exchange on trading platforms and housing markets. The effect of this reached a peak with the financial collapse in 2008, when the bursting of the sub-prime bubble showed the weak fundamentals of the system we created.

Now this capacity to automate automation is bringing a completely new dimension to the dynamics between labour and capital, which we need to address to understand the scale of the disruption AI is going to bring.

Some think of AI in purely optimistic terms, imagining that tech will ultimately turn against capital, by facilitating a change in the way we live, with people being able to automate work, thus being able to indulge in much more interesting and creative activities.

This may sound good, but they are missing a key point: this new form of immaterial labour, the automation of automation, is possible only within the realm of large corporations and the products they produce.

This is where we need politics. Unless we challenge the business model we are in, we won't be able to deal with the consequences of AI on the labour market.

In the United States, for example, a master's graduate in data science (likely to be male) can earn over $100,000 a year,[82] while a ghost worker earns a quarter of that. The accumulation of power in the big corporations and the commodities they produce remains uncontested, and to challenge it we would need to drastically reform their business model (based on our time, our money, our data), which we are not yet prepared to do.

We have seen how disconnected the political world is from the reality of data as capital, and it will require an immense shift in public thinking to achieve the change we need. Those who think the political answer to tech economics is redistribution are misleading themselves and the public: with both traditional automation and the automation of automation, jobs are inevitably going to be lost. So the answer has to be the reform of the business model, one that really treats data as a new form of capital.

Finally, what is also different now is the absence of intermediaries. Two centuries ago, with the industrial revolution, trade unions were formed to act as intermediaries. Their role was to stand between the needs of the owners of the business and those of the workers. However, in an age of atomized workers and zero-hours contracts, one could argue that trade unions are becoming increasingly less relevant.

Some liberal thinkers think it is necessary to promote the role of consumers and to nurture new forms of solidarity between them, with consumer politics replacing the producer politics of trade unionism. I often hear this at round table discussions with business leaders around the world. They argue that a new sovereignty needs to be established, one of consumer rights.

As a feminist, I profoundly disagree with this view. I realized long ago that women were better off in a trade union, especially when it comes to maternity pay and other crucial rights, although admittedly there has always been more trade unionism in the feminism movement than feminism in the trade union movement. It is not a zero sum game: trade unions and consumer rights are both vitally important functions of modern democracies, and need to be strengthened across the board, rather than completely rethought.

Consumers play a key role, and I certainly realize that they can make ethical choices, thus driving businesses, choices, accountability and transparency. However, over recent years, it has only been thanks to the bravery of whistle-blowers and former employees of tech organizations that knowledge of the devastating effects of the unaccountable use of AI is in the public domain.

We have already discussed the Cambridge Analytica story coming to light thanks to Christopher Wylie, Shahmir Sanni, Brittany Kaiser and reporter Carole Cadwalladr. In the United States, the Google Walkout (led by Meredith Whittaker, who was subsequently dismissed and joined the AI Now Institute, home to some of the most interesting thinking around the ethics of tech) brought into the public domain the disillusioning reality of abuse within Google, such as forced arbitration for sexual harassment and assault cases.[83] Sadly, accountability is too often left to researchers to flag a problem.

At the moment, good AI seems to be narrated by the PR departments of big companies, and bad AI by the whistle-blowers.

If we are to trust these new technologies, structures need to be in place for workers to ensure that the products they are developing are not used to damage democracy, for surveillance or, say, in the service of separating children from their families at US borders.[84] We should remember that Amazon workers rebelled when they found out their company was selling facial-recognition software to Palantir, a data-analytics company that is under public scrutiny for its technical support of US immigration enforcement practices and for the lack of privacy measures in its cooperation with police departments.[85]

In *Now We Have Your Attention: The New Politics of the People*, journalist Jack Shenker reflects on how gig-economy workers are using tech to fight back, and how new apps allow workers to get organized for protests, to record wrongdoings and abuse by management, and to stage sit-ins.[86]

Time and time again in my discussions about the impact of AI and automation on work, the conversation comes around to how women are likely, yet again, to be at the sharp end of another disruptive change. This is not just because it is probable that a lot of jobs in sectors traditionally dominated by women, especially retail, will disappear. The impact will vary and will depend on countries and economies. For example, Masego Madzwamuse, CEO at the Southern Africa Trust, is right that we worry a lot about job losses within formal labour markets. But in Africa, she says, the bulk of women work in the informal economy, which makes a contribution to GDP of somewhere between 30 per cent and 40 per cent.[87] As AI is likely to affect that sector, she asks what will happen to the right and the capacity of women to participate in the economy, and their right to derive equitable benefits from innovation. The reality is, as she puts it, that 'there is a lot of value in how the informal economy is organized, the solidarity, the dependence on social relations and the fact that the benefits are accrued to the household level where they are most needed'.

There won't be a one-size-fits-all way to deal with job replacement, but one thing is striking. Women have fought for centuries for the right to work and still fight for equal pay. Recent statistics show that, across the EU, women's gross hourly earnings were on average 16 per cent below those of men, with the highest wage gap recorded in Estonia (25.6 per cent) and the lowest in Romania (3.5 per cent).[88] Women still lag behind men at the top of companies and governments alike. After all this struggle, we are now told that we are replaceable – unless we go into coding.

Countless organizations advocating for more women in tech are appearing. Don't get me wrong – this really is excellent news, as we desperately need more women in technology. It's unacceptable that less than one quarter of the workforce in AI is female.[89] But the point is that, once again, it falls upon us to sort out our own problems.

Tech culture is not very friendly to women. For example, what message does it send that, as I write, MIT has been brought into disrepute for yet another example of big tech institutions cutting corners in ethics at the expense of women? The head of the MIT Media Lab, Joichi Ito, was forced to resign following revelations about the academic centre's financial ties to Jeffrey Epstein, a convicted child sex offender.[90] Ito and other Media Lab staff continued to accept contributions from

Epstein after his first conviction in 2008 and actively tried to conceal where these contributions came from.

If the techno-elites behave like this, how can they expect to be trusted by female colleagues? The dramatic and damaging lack of diversity cannot be a surprise if this is the culture underpinning it.

AI is both a fact and an ideology. More women need to take up science and coding, and the infantilization of women in the tech realm is a cultural product that has nothing to do with biology. But if we want to address the future of humanity and AI, what we desperately need is more women in politics and at the top of institutions, to govern and drive change.

6

WHY DON'T WE HAVE AN ANTI-AI MOVEMENT?

I often ask myself this question, because I think it would be useful to inject a new dimension into the debate and to force a change of pace. Right now, we continue to automate inequalities by embedding social hierarchies into machines governing more and more aspects of our lives. We need a more nuanced debate, and a pause.

To begin with, how do we decide whether tech is better equipped than a human to perform a specific task? Currently, our thinking is dominated by what Meredith Broussard, who posed that question, calls technochauvinism, which is the presumption that the most technologically advanced solution is, necessarily, the best one.[91]

We are all taking part in an AI race, without really knowing what is waiting for us at the finishing line. The consensus is that tech is good and is improving our lives, starting with healthcare and moving into every other realm, but that, at the same time, there are unresolved issues around privacy and human dignity. When new challenges emerge, such as the downsides of the gig economy in terms of rights and security in work, or unaccountable facial-recognition systems being used on our streets without our knowledge, or workers having to use wearables tracking their productivity around the clock, the legitimacy of these technologies is questioned, with long-term consequences in relation to trust as well as productivity. It is time for the force of the law to intervene.

AI is transformative: its application impacts across all industries, reshapes the essence of labour and is in effect a geopolitical arsenal that transforms global relationships. AI is much more than technology: it is about power – the power to disrupt our democratic processes and create turmoil by replacing jobs with machines.

All around the world, countries are equipping themselves with the best resources to produce AI systems. Finland has started to train its population in coding. The UK has set up an Office for Artificial Intelligence and a Centre for Data Ethics and Innovation, and the European Union has established myriad initiatives to grow AI and to further academic as well as business work in the field.

Right now, China and the United States are leading the way, and that is where most of the innovation is happening, and it is worth reflecting on this.

These two countries have very different models. The Chinese state has created its own companies, harvesting the data of its citizens throughout their daily lives. China is also, allegedly, far ahead in 5G and well placed for the development of quantum technologies. The United States invests trillions in its AI systems and has far fewer restrictions on the use of personal data, although the landscape is changing, with a proliferation of recent legislation covering privacy and even the accountability of algorithms.[92]

The nine largest companies dominating the digital world are all based in either China or the United States: Baidu, Alibaba Group Holding Limited and Tencent in China, and Google, Microsoft, Amazon, Facebook, IBM and Apple in the United States. Given that AI is about data, and data concerns the digital, the same companies that dominate the digital environment are also the ones directing the debate around AI innovation.

While the United States and China compete for global AI superiority, with the media reporting on the sci-fi elements of both countries' advances, Europe is also nurturing AI talent and innovation. The focus of the EU, however, is ethics. I will go on to further address AI ethics, but, for now, one point is essential. Even the ethics of AI is not immune from the international race. Regulation of AI is to an extent the only 'weapon' Europe has to compete with at a global level, and that is because Europe does not have the same approach to data exploitation as China and the United States.

In China, the approach is rather totalitarian, with citizen data collected and used on the basis of a state-led approach. In the United States, data is exploited on a market-led basis, where consumer data is easily accessible, including credit and financial information. In the EU, privacy is viewed as a matter of the dignity of the individual, thus necessitating restrictions on the sharing and manipulation of data. For Europe, regulating AI means setting out what it feels is an ethical way to deploy this technology, but it also means establishing rules and standards that the rest of the world would inevitably have to comply with to trade globally.

The reality is that AI innovation, as we have seen, holds enormous promise, but, if unregulated, we are likely to cede more power to already powerful companies. It is unlikely that any other organization will have more searches than Google, or that any marketplace will be bigger than Amazon – unless, of course, they are broken up, or unless regulation diminishes their power by, for example, imposing a radical change to the digital advertising ecosystem, which would inevitably challenge the business models of Google and Facebook.

To put it simply: from the standpoint of both privacy and competition, regulation needs to be viewed as the path to power, and it would be naive to disguise this element in our analysis.

Considering AI as a global race is disconcerting because we are talking about technologies that will drastically change our human experience and redefine labour as we know it. Going back to the original question, why don't we have an anti-AI movement in the way that we had (and still have) an anti-nuclear movement? AI is not that different in the sense that its use for military purposes is considerable. The military application of AI has made great strides in recent years, with automated weapons now able to target and shoot without human intervention.[93]

The Joint Artificial Intelligence Center at the Pentagon has seen its 2020 budget rise from $93 million to $268 million. This renewed focus comes at a time when there are 'fears that China has gained an early advantage in the global race to explore AI's military potential, including for command and control and autonomous weapons'.[94]

As with nuclear power, AI needs huge funding, and its development is driven by the global race and dynamics between superpower nation states. The international community has accepted that nuclear energy has positive, transformative qualities, alongside its dangers, meaning that it needs to be controlled by a centralized hierarchical chain of command. So the question is: since AI possesses both incredibly beneficial elements (think, again, of healthcare) together with chilling risks (manipulation, control and the devaluing of labour), why aren't we considering a similar degree of authoritarian oversight in the form of binding agreements and international conventions safeguarding humanity?

There are two answers to this question. The first lies with a simple lack of awareness. Despite recent data scandals, including Cambridge Analytica, showing what happens when software hoovers up the digital space, the narrative around AI is too focused on the implications of the existence of highly advanced robots in the future, rather than around the more urgent question of what AI is doing now.

The second is that some of the most troubling effects of AI concern women, and women's voices are still largely unheard – not just because few women are in coding (generally speaking, since there are discrepancies across different parts of the world), but also because too few are in politics and at the helm of governments, in positions that will shape the future of innovation.

An example of how disconcerting AI is for women is Sophia, the female-looking humanoid robot.[95] Sophia is slim, white and has behavioural intelligence, which means she can smile, joke and respond to an individual's tone of voice. Humans refer to Sophia as 'she', and Saudi Arabia – a country, let us not forget, where women are barely able to drive without male permission[96] – has even granted it citizenship. This is only the beginning and it should be an issue for us all.

The final reason why the danger of AI is underestimated is the dominance of the big companies, who are setting the parameters of the debate. Ultimately, we are looking in terms of numbers and figures to determine what is – and isn't – desirable. Efficiency, for example, is generally considered positive. AI enables us to speed up human tasks, and this is seen as a good outcome. When looking at the effect on jobs, the usual view is that, yes, there will be disruption, but more jobs will be created. When you question this logic, even when you also believe in the possibilities of AI, you are labelled anti-technology and, by extension, anti-progress, anti-modernity.

Think again of nuclear energy. Does the insistence on rigorous regulation of atomic energy make one anti-progress? Or does it make one a responsible individual, aware of the inherent risks of technology while still aware of the potential benefits of this technology if used properly?

But international agreements and relevant worthwhile debates require institutions within which these negotiations can happen. We only need look at the global #MeToo movement or the school strike for the climate campaigns or more localized uprisings from Hong Kong to Sudan to know that the increased confidence of social movements is coinciding with a crisis of legitimacy and trust in many of our established institutions.

While the power of global social movements is encouraging, the lack of trust in our institutions is problematic, because regulating and governing AI requires the force of the law and strong cooperative diplomatic relationships between nations, rather than competition.

7

OPPRESSION
AND RESISTANCE

In 2019, I travelled to China to deliver a speech at the UNESCO International Conference on Artificial Intelligence and Education. It gathered business leaders and ministers from around the world under the UN umbrella to determine how AI can improve education, whether in smart classrooms or through individually tailored education, based on the needs, personality and abilities of the student. Such personalized education can use AI to analyse how a student responds to different pedagogical approaches to identify the most effective methodology for them.

The delegates were enthusiastic and willing to discuss limits and boundaries. Many countries – including China, Namibia, Russia and Argentina – agreed that AI should augment, not replace, teachers and that AI should also be ethical and respect humanity. Interestingly, the Chinese minister for education highlighted how new technologies have enabled the country to lift many out of poverty and illiteracy.

However, by the end of the conference, once the principles had been approved, with humanity, ethics and the social good at the very heart of them, it seemed that no newspaper had reported on it. Instead, the next day, the *China Daily* dedicated three pages to a large event in Shenzhen at which world business leaders discussed the practical applications of AI... with no ethics in sight.

Reading those pages as I left Beijing, I felt, once again, that the arena of AI ethics was an important place to be – but that merely occupying that space was not enough. Ethics is critical. There is nothing neutral about AI, its development, its use and the selection of data that its algorithms are fed. Exchanging pleasantries about ethics is useless if what we really want is for those global business leaders in Shenzhen to transform their companies' use of AI.

If we do not establish such regulation now, we will soon come to regret it. The big tech companies were harvesting our data while privacy law was still in its infancy, and we are already seeing the consequences and paying the price for our inaction.

The connection between AI and corporate power is already solid, and we see it in the link between academia and corporations involved in AI.[97] The 2018 AI Index statistics show that the number of corporate-affiliated AI papers has grown significantly in recent years.[98] The start-up scene is also vibrant, with most new companies supported by venture-capital firms, which themselves then hope to be hoovered up by big tech.

AI ethics is not immune to the close relationship with corporate power either. We have seen a proliferation of principles, guidance, processes and frameworks established by big corporations to reassure consumers that they take an ethical approach to innovation (whether or not they actually do).[99] There is a lot of discussion surrounding the ethics of AI, and the terminology that goes along with this is as enticing as it is pompous: trustworthy AI, responsible AI, ethical AI, AI for good.

The idea prevails that AI needs to be ethical and respond to normative tenets that we, society, determine as being beneficial to us and for the progress of the world we inhabit.

Thousands of people, myself included, have dedicated their professional careers to advocating for more ethical AI practices, but how many more conferences do we need to restate these principles, to once again recognize fairness and argue that algorithms are biased and so need to be fixed? I wrote this book expressly to go beyond that. Ethical tourism feels superficially good, but what purpose does it really serve?

Now, when I attend round tables and events to discuss the intended and unintended consequences of AI, I often hear fears around facial recognition, surveillance and control – and the finger gets pointed at China, and often only at China. We know China is developing the Orwellian 'Social Credit System', which should be in place by the end of 2020.

China's Social Credit System rates citizens on their trustworthiness and adherence to rules, including speed limits. There are many systems, not one, and they are operated by companies like Sesame Credit, the financial arm of Alibaba. To calculate the scores, these systems require a high degree of surveillance, gathering citizen data through social media, smartphones and any connected devices. All this information is then churned through algorithms that work out individual scores. The city of Rongcheng, for example, gives all residents 1,000 points, and authorities make deductions for bad behaviour such as going through red traffic lights, and add points for charity donations or similar examples of good behaviour.

Through the use of facial recognition, people do not need to be reported or referred for bad or good behaviour; this happens automatically. Allegedly, a lot of acts of kindness are already being seen in the streets – acts that citizens hope will be caught on camera, thus increasing their scores. What citizens get in return for compliant behaviour is higher-achieving schools for their kids, priority for housing assignments and similar privileges. The system is therefore based on three things: social control (or surveillance), reward and punishment. This is not new in China: of the ten cities in the world with the highest number of CCTV cameras, nine are Chinese. (The tenth is London.)

China has created a deeply penetrative surveillance state, and we hear reports about how DNA-, voice- and facial-recognition technology is used to track and target the mostly Muslim Uighurs, a minority in China but the biggest group in Xinjiang, China's largest and westernmost region. It is reported that at least one million Uighurs are detained in what Beijing calls re-education camps, although some human-rights groups have defined them as concentration camps.[100]

However, pointing the finger at the Chinese is naive and narrow-minded, because they did not create all of this in isolation. The Americans – some knowingly, some unwittingly – have helped advance this system. As *The Intercept* magazine reported, the

OpenPower Foundation – a non-profit led by Google and IBM executives with the aim of trying to 'drive innovation' – has set up a collaboration between IBM, Chinese company Semptian, and US chip-manufacturer Xilinx. Together, they have worked to advance a breed of microprocessors that enable computers to analyse vast amounts of data more efficiently.[101]

This is the context of the ethics debate: despite the nationalist mood of the time, big tech is mobile, and global.

Consider this: in a public discussion with Arkady Volozh, the CEO of Yandex, about AI, Russian President Vladimir Putin asserted that 'whoever becomes the leader in this sphere will become the ruler of the world'.[102] Elon Musk later shared Putin's words on Twitter, adding, 'Competition for AI superiority at the national level most likely cause of WW3.'[103]

So how will ethics fit into this global race? Will it be used only as a soporific, to lull consumers into a passive state when it comes to emergent technology? And the big question must never be overlooked: what is AI actually for in the first place? Without considering this question, we are not challenging the brutal power dynamics that underpin AI.

Look at the impact that home technology has had on the lives of women. Many argue that dishwashers and hoovers were instrumental in liberating women from time-consuming household chores. But have domestic machinery and now tech really helped women escape the home realm? Isn't the opposite true, that the narrative of tech as empowerment has been turned against women to continue imprisoning us into accepting a disproportionate burden of housework?[104] Are smart fridges that tell us when we have run out of butter really reducing the strain on women? And the same for devices that clean automatically and super-efficiently? These are questions that we must ask ourselves as the statistics show that women are still allotted more house-cleaning responsibilities than men. Haven't the expectations placed on women just become higher? Has house tech not merely become another device to keep women in the house in a modernized version of their traditional caregiving roles?

This is all because the answer to structural inequality is a political and not a technological one, and technology, in itself, does not prevent us from reiterating pre-existing power hierarchies. This is not to say that tech cannot help – quite the opposite. The real challenge, however, is understanding what tech is for and who it is there to serve.

In July 2019, when the British Conservative MP and Secretary of State for Health and Social Care Matt Hancock announced the deployment of Alexa 'to allow elderly people, blind people and other patients who cannot easily search for health advice on the internet to access the information through the voice-powered voice assistant',[105] the news was widely welcomed. The argument was that we can train Alexa on the information provided on the NHS Direct website (medical information that helps assess whether or not to seek urgent help), so that patients can instantly ask the software for information and avoid going directly to the overstretched, state-funded doctor. The undeniable truth is that the British National Health Service is chronically underfunded, and the dismantling of public services has been a feature of our society – and many others – in recent years.

Technology can help in reducing inefficiency and paperwork, as well as improving diagnosis. But the NHS is also a realm of technochauvinism. I went on the BBC in July 2019, and, while I praised the idea of technological innovation in a healthcare system that definitely needs improving, I did question whether the ethical impact of this had been thoroughly considered.

As just one concern among many, what about the thousands of women who suffer domestic abuse daily, or the two women who die every week at the hands of angry men, partners and husbands? A doctor's practice may be one of the few escape routes or 'excuses' for an entrapped woman to leave the house. She might go for something unrelated to her abuse and, in the relative safe space of a doctor's clinic, confide her domestic suffering. Or someone could ask the right question, and a single question, asked by people who are trained at spotting the signs of abuse, may well offer a lifeline for many women. Let's not forget that male violence is as serious a cause of death and incapacity for women worldwide as cancer, above malaria, road accidents and war.[106]

Considerations around ethics, to be really transformative, must start by challenging whose ethics we are actually talking about. This book insists that we need to talk about power. The ethics we are discussing must shift the parameters of society as it is now. Our current position with AI reminds me of the marches of feminists in the 1960s and 1970s where women were demanding the right to abortion with the defiant call to arms, 'Whose body? My body!' Now, our drumbeat is, 'Whose AI? My AI!'

The consensus now, at least in the West, seems to be that ethics needs to be taught on computer engineering degrees so that coders appreciate the complexity of the issue.

Let's think of a real case involving so-called bias. A Microsoft customer was testing a financial-services algorithm that did risk-scoring for loans. They spotted that the model was favouring men. The problem was that as the developers were training the data set, the data was historical, taken from all previously approved loans. As most of the people who had applied for loans with their personal information had been men, the algorithm drew the conclusion that men posed a lower risk.[107]

Conscientious developers can make the active choice to mitigate the risk of gender discrimination by removing all clues about gender from every CV. However, it is more complex than this as other forms of discrimination can, and do, still arise – in relation to postcodes, for example. Postcodes are not just places where people live; postcodes can signal socio-economic background, ethnicity, even sexual orientation (think of a particularly gay-friendly area, for instance). This is to say that the difficulty of tackling the unintended consequences that algorithms are bringing is an enormous task, as algorithms reflect the structural problems of our societies.

Teaching technical solutions to these problems would never solve the problem entirely.

The fact that there is a whole movement working around standards, benchmarks and all sorts of auditable criteria to incorporate into product development, and check against, should not come as a surprise either. Confirming compliance will be beneficial but also shifts responsibility. While useful, compliance does not solve the substantial structural issues underpinning the AI industry.

In theory, we could have a product that meets all the standards and is totally unbiased but is still deployed for the wrong reasons. Or we could have new products that appear progressive but are based on bogus science, products whose deployment could lead to dangerous, unintended consequences.

As I write, it appears that Facebook is funding research on brain-computer interfaces that can pick up thoughts directly from our neurons and translate them into words. The researchers involved claim that they have an algorithm that is already able to do this.[108] In 1984, George Orwell wrote that, 'Nothing was your own concept except the few cubic centimetres around your skull.' Well, Facebook and Neuralink seem to suggest that this sequestered space may too become an exposed part of the public domain. Other companies are doing the same, making us think that the last frontier of privacy – our own brain – may one day disappear.

Apart from the fact that many may question the legitimacy of the science behind these claims, what – and whose – interest would these brain-computer interfaces serve? And where will these technologies take us without tight controls? Some argue that paralysed patients could benefit from implants capable of reading directly from their brains, allowing them to perform activities they otherwise couldn't. However, the risks of these technologies are immense, and frameworks need to be established before moving forward.

Another example of such dubious science is the AI lie detector funded by the European Union. The product, called iBorderCtrl, is allegedly in use at checkpoints in Hungary, Greece and Latvia.[109] Scientists and academics have long criticized these 'deception identifier tools' for being pseudoscientific and likely to lead to unfair outcomes for individuals.[110]

How necessary and ethical is a lie detector in any situation? We could theoretically construct a completely unbiased lie detector. The question remains: what would make its use ethical? That is not just a judgement for ethics classrooms – this is a political argument. No surprise given that AI is, as we have established, about power, so we must deal with it politically.

For women, being political means interrogating the essential nature of the inequalities that AI is at risk of embedding even further. MIT, in an attempt to teach ethics to engineering students, recently proposed a curriculum comprised of Aristotle, Machiavelli, Bacon, Hobbes, Locke, the Founding Fathers and the Bible.[111] Can you spot the problem?

8

THE ETHICS INDUSTRY

Oppression can be defined as a situation where bias held against a section of people becomes elevated to general wisdom, with social and human rights denied to them as a result, whether this be implicitly or explicitly. We have seen how AI underpins online manipulation, social control and the radical transformation of labour. We have looked at how ignorance around the risks plays into the hands of companies inundating the market with often inaccurate products with little accountability and oversight. These products progressively software us out, make decisions for us, decide whether we are allowed a visa, a loan or a job interview. All this relies on us not noticing, not understanding and thus, not challenging.

So the crucial question arises for women worldwide: is AI simply going to encode oppression by embedding it even further as every aspect of our lives is progressively taken over by software? The 'matrix of domination', a phrase coined by academic Patricia Hill Collins, demonstrates how class, race and gender are interlocking systems, so those who find themselves at the intersections are hit hardest.[112] The truth of this is well illustrated by the fact, already discussed, that AI-driven facial-recognition systems do not work on black women, or in the way that AI is used to tighten social control around poorer and more vulnerable citizens.

Neither the zeitgeist around ethics nor the rallying cry for there to be more women in technology is sufficient to alter the alarming direction it is taking. That is because it is so easy to cut corners when it comes to ethics.

Ethics, as philosopher Luciano Floridi explains, is increasingly at risk of turning into 'ethics bluewashing', where ethical principles are established to justify and further commercial aims, and not the other way around.[113] The proliferation of ethical tools, often under the umbrella of the same large organizations that have dubious privacy practices, does make people wonder how sincere those efforts are, even whether they are a cynical ploy to distract consumers' attention from the truth.

'I'd blush if I could.' That is how, until recently, Alexa responded to being called a 'bitch'.[114] Social pressure and international outrage finally made Amazon change this default response, but, despite a last-minute patch, the problem of female-gendered interfaces remains.

There are strong commercial incentives behind choosing characters and creating artefacts that the user might feel more comfortable conversing with, thus encouraging engagement and accelerating the accumulation of data. Perhaps, technology artefacts are given a female identity to help seduce a user into thinking it is pliable and benign. Seductive and flirtatious Alexa, Siri and Cortana all have female names. They are there to serve, support and help us with all our activities.

Our five-year-old boys grow up thinking that it is normal to have a female ready, at all times, to serve you, and our little girls may perhaps find it natural to think that this digital servitude extends to the real world.

Once, I was talking about this on the radio, and the presenter interrupted, sounding exasperated, 'What do you have against the fact that people trust female voices, and find them more reassuring?' Here is the problem: the female cyborg – whether Alexa or Sophia, the robot with 'empathy' – smiles and supports but is not entitled to challenge, and that is why it is considered reassuring. The female cyborg obeys.

We have not moved far from Galatea, Pygmalion's beloved statue, and perhaps the prototype of today's sex robots. It should alarm us all that a 2017 survey showed that 40 per cent of men were considering buying a sex doll in the next five years.[115] The reasons vary, from sexual aids to loneliness and social anxiety, with 11 per cent admitting they prefer dolls as a replacement for a human.[116]

Samantha is a smart sex doll. It responds to human touch, is blonde and skinny and has sensual lips. When it was introduced at the Ars Electronica Festival in Linz, Austria, in 2017, showcasing the developments in animatronics and AI to make sex dolls ever more lifelike, Samantha didn't remain intact for long. Men explored the doll so aggressively that its body was ruptured in several places. Think about this for a moment: the objectification of a female-looking body exposed and available for males to savage.[117]

In 2017, a company in California produced Harmony, a prototype hyper-realistic sex robot that can tell jokes, quote Shakespeare and remember birthdays. It can also hold a conversation about music, movies and books. And, of course, Harmony will have sex whenever its owner demands.[118]

Unsurprisingly, smart-doll brothels are popping up in quite a few locations. KinkySdollS, a Canadian firm, attempted to launch in Houston as part of a US expansion. Opposition from the mayor and from Christian groups meant that the project was eventually halted.[119]

It has been argued that sex robots will curb the trafficking of women and girls,[120] but as of yet there is no evidence for this argument. What is far more likely is that this form of 3D pornography will only increase women's subjugation and the violence of men's sexual fantasies. The point here is that the more sophisticated these artefacts become (owing to the progress in animatronics and AI), the more difficult it will be to eliminate their gendering and sexualization.

The, now familiar, answer seems to be that we need more women in technology. I think this is right – but also misleading. There is no doubt that the relationship between women and technology has been complex over the years, and I feel some sympathy for those who have been reluctant to engage with tech as a conscious or unconscious response to military and scientific abuses within the patriarchal system.

A couple of years ago, I flew to Sweden to address coders and developers on the opportunities and challenges of AI. I remember being shocked at the sight of how male-dominated the audience was in the country of Pippi Longstocking and a statutory full year of paid paternity leave. I remember debating these issues at a conference and someone raising an interesting point of view: that the most gender-equal nations, places like Sweden, with comparatively more women in politics and on company boards, have a lower number of women in tech, as in these places women can exercise choice and focus on something more inherently feminine like art and creative occupations.

While some find this theory attractive, it is clear to me that the reason for this imbalance has more to do with culture and, in particular, with the binary Western approach to the world: women as emotional and irrational; men as rational, thus numerical. Women have disappeared from the history of computing with the relatively recent professionalization and managerialization of coding.

It wasn't always thus: women were in computing when it was viewed as an extension of secretarial work; women were at Bletchley Park, working with Alan Turing and computing manually what is now done by machines. Performing those complex computations was perhaps viewed as scarcely different to the methodical work of a secretary, and women, used to embroidery and knitting and the precision and patience that these tasks require, were considered perfect for this, too.

At some point, with powerful coding machines being introduced by companies like IBM, humans were no longer needed to compute – complex machines could do that for them. That is when the number of women started to progressively decrease. This didn't occur by chance. The higher-status computational work remaining was taken over by male managers.

Computing was replaced by the commodification of data, soon to be turning into capital – the logic of accumulation once again favouring men. The culture of the programming environment didn't suit women: testosterone has been, and remains, dominant.

A recently circulated internal document has exposed that one year after Google staff's #MeToo walkout, little has changed.[121] In November 2018, 20,000 employees around the world walked out of Google's offices in protest at the revelation that the company had paid out over $100 million to multiple executives accused of sexual harassment.[122] At the time, the company apologized profusely, saying that it would overhaul its policies and make Google a safe place to work.

A year later, employees spoke of being silenced, of suffering retaliation and of still being too worried to officially report any harassment. This culture is not uncommon in the tech sector and is a problem that is putting women off entering it. This is important as we grapple with the need for more women in technology to design the tools that are shaping so much of our lives today.

Perhaps structural defects leading to bias and algorithmic racism would not happen with a diverse workforce, one that looks at the intended and perhaps unintended consequences of a product when deployed in our world. More women of colour in coding would surely mean that greater attention would be placed on data sets, processes and possibly distorted outcomes discriminating against whole sections of our society.

However, we cannot and must not let ourselves be fooled that as long as women are in the operating room then everything is going to be fine. AI is far more than technology, and it is way beyond technology that we must set our sights if this is not to be yet another setback for women from every walk of life.

CONCLUSION

POLITICAL ARTEFACTS
NEED POLITICAL ANSWERS

AI has an unrivalled potential to transform future and present societies, but it is also related to oppression. And if we can understand how AI is related to oppression, then we can understand how to resist it.

Oppression happens on a number of levels: online manipulation fuelling women-degrading and feminist-hating populism; social control and the tightening of data extraction around the most vulnerable and those visibly requiring help from government; and the transformation of labour, making traditional policies of redistribution obsolete.

With all this in mind, we need to understand that norms, values and assumptions are encoded into AI and data-driven systems. In the words of academic Langdon Winner, 'artifacts can have political qualities... In our times, people are often willing to make drastic changes in the way they live to accord with technological innovation at the same time they would resist similar kinds of changes justified on political grounds.'[123]

Artefacts have politics because they are fed data, and data is not neutral. But it is not only about data. It is about the fact that the use of AI right now seems to be focused on punishment rather than reward or social progress. The choice of what an artefact is going to be used for is a political one – and it often relates to the oppression that we have talked about throughout this book.

Therefore, familiarizing ourselves with the politics of AI and challenging the sanctity of data and data-driven decisions are important acts of resistance.

The same goes for online recommendations, especially when they are calculated by 'clustering', a process of categorizing individuals into clusters of people with similar interests and similar behaviour. This process is called collaborative filtering, and it is the biggest risk our society is facing in relation to the preservation and nurturing of our autonomy of choice as well as our democratic values. Clustering individuals into groups of 'similars' means social stereotypes are only going to be reproduced and further reinforced through echo chambers and filter bubbles.

We need to be able to interrogate and defy the process of being softwared out in our daily lives, and we need to work on a collective level. Technology has never been presented to women in a nuanced way. Over the decades, new tools have been introduced as either something that will solve all problems, or as something that will ultimately destroy our rights and freedoms.

The risk we are facing right now is the power of oppression from the AI artefacts used for surveillance, manipulation and control. They are reaffirming the same power structures we have been trying to abolish over the last centuries.

But there is a way out. And the way out is, certainly, to code better – more fairly, more democratically – but it is also to be able to see AI as part of a bigger political and geopolitical picture. To put it simply, we can make sure that facial-recognition software does not discriminate, but that does not mean that facial recognition should be used in the first place. We need to ask searching questions about how we govern the use, research and deployment of one of the most transformative tools the world has ever seen – and particularly so considering the technology is developing rapidly at a time of heightened turbulence, populism, social inequality and breakdown in trust of traditional political structures.

Hope may be found in the emergence of a younger generation, especially young women, such as climate justice activist Greta Thunberg, who are changing consciousness through being global voices on the important issues that define humanity: the environment, the anti-slavery movement, ethics, equality, anti-corruption campaigns and freedom of speech. And it is not by chance that when Greta speaks, she is answered by a roar of misogynist nastiness, largely coming from allegedly grown men in both Europe and the United States.

Obviously, these kinds of attacks on her have no basis in fact. Thunberg's views on climate change align with those of 97 per cent of climate scientists.[124] But research shows that environmentalism is indeed perceived as a feminine issue – so the sexist bullying with which Greta is battered should come as no surprise.

As political institutions look increasingly obsolete, and nationalisms prevail, a new global agenda is being shaped outside the traditional political avenues. It is predicated on a different approach to power that needs to underpin how we harness AI and its potential for the future of the planet. To do so, AI needs accountability, scrutiny and global norms wrapped around it, with the same seriousness that we bring to debates around nuclear power.

Amid the global turmoil, maybe, just maybe, the promise of the Artificial will force us to confront our shared humanity and the physical and digital environments we inhabit. For many of us, disappointed yet optimistic, this is the time to dare to imagine.

REFERENCES

1   European Commission High-Level Expert Group on Artificial
     Intelligence, 'Policy and Investment Recommendations for
     Trustworthy AI', European Commission (26 Jun. 2019),
     https://ec.europa.eu/newsroom/dae/document.cfm?doc_
     id=60343, accessed 23 Dec. 2019.
2   Leah Fessler, 'We tested bots like Siri and Alexa to see who
     would stand up to sexual harassment', *Quartz* (22 Feb. 2017),
     https://qz.com/911681/we-tested-apples-siri-amazon-echos-
     alexa-microsofts-cortana-and-googles-google-home-to-see-
     which-personal-assistant-bots-stand-up-for-themselves-in-
     the-face-of-sexual-harassment, accessed 9 Dec. 2019.
3   Clare McDonald, 'Less than a quarter of AI professionals
     are women', *Computer Weekly* (21 Dec. 2018), https://www.
     computerweekly.com/news/252454841/Less-than-a-quarter-
     of-AI-professionals-are-women, accessed 23 Dec. 2019.
4   Victoria Turk, 'Home robot to nudge older people to stay social and
     active', *New Scientist* (11 Jan. 2017), https://www.newscientist.
     com/article/mg23331084-000-home-assistant-robot-to-nudge-
     elderly-to-stay-social-and-active/#ixzz6AempCMFj, accessed
     11 Jan. 2020.

5   Luke Stangel, 'Silicon Valley's 10 highest-paid CEOs of 2018 may not be who you'd expect', *Silicon Valley Business Journal* (12 Apr. 2018), https://www.bizjournals.com/sanjose/news/2018/04/12/these-are-silicon-valley-s-10-highest-paid-ceos-of.html, accessed 8 Sep. 2019.

6   Cade Metz, 'AI Is Learning from Humans. Many Humans', *New York Times* (16 Aug. 2019), https://www.nytimes.com/2019/08/16/technology/ai-humans.html, accessed 13 Dec. 2019.

7   Ibid.

8   Casey Newton, 'The Trauma Floor: The Secret Lives of Facebook Moderators in America', *The Verge* (25 Feb. 2019), https://www.theverge.com/2019/2/25/18229714/cognizant-facebook-content-moderator-interviews-trauma-working-conditions-arizona, accessed 20 Jan. 2020.

9   Nicola Crose and Moh Musa, 'The new assembly lines: Why AI needs low-skilled workers too', *World Economic Forum* (12 Aug. 2019), https://www.weforum.org/agenda/2019/08/ai-low-skilled-workers/, accessed 22 Jan. 2020.

10 Angela Chen, 'How Silicon Valley's successes are fueled by an underclass of "ghost workers"', *The Verge* (13 May 2019), https://www.theverge.com/2019/5/13/18563284/mary-gray-ghost-work-microwork-labor-silicon-valley-automation-employment-interview, accessed 13 Dec. 2019.

11 Colin Lecher, 'Google employees "refuse to be complicit" in border agency cloud contract', *The Verge* (14 Aug. 2019), https://www.theverge.com/2019/8/14/20805432/google-employees-petition-protest-customs-border-cloud-computing-contract, accessed 13 Nov. 2019.

12 Bernard Marr, 'How Much Data Do We Create Every Day? The Mind-Blowing Stats Everyone Should Read', *Forbes* (21 May 2018), https://www.forbes.com/sites/bernardmarr/2018/05/21/how-much-data-do-we-create-every-day-the-mind-blowing-stats-everyone-should-read/#50673b5460ba, accessed 23 Dec. 2019.

13 M. Rovatsos, B. Mittelstadt, A. Koene, Centre for Data Ethics and Innovation, 'Landscape Summary: Bias in Algorithmic Decision-Making', https://assets.publishing.service.gov.uk/government/uploads/system/uploads/attachment_data/

file/819055/Landscape_Summary_-_Bias_in_Algorithmic_ Decision-Making.pdf, accessed 20 Jan. 2020.

14 Rebecca Taylor, 'Teenager "tweets from smart fridge after mother confiscates her phone"', *Sky News* (15 Aug. 2019), https://news.sky.com/story/teenager-tweets-from-smart-fridge-after-mother-confiscates-her-phone-11785107, accessed 13 Dec. 2019.

15 A. Huntington and J.A. Gilmour, 'A life shaped by pain: women and endometriosis', *Journal of Clinical Nursing*, 14/9 (2005), 1124-1132. doi: 10.1111/j.1365-2702.2005.01231.x,

16 C. Morassutto et al., 'Incidence and Estimated Prevalence of Endometriosis and Adenomyosis in Northeast Italy: A Data Linkage Study', *PLOS One*, 11/4 (2016), 11-11. doi: 10.1371/journal.pone.0154227

17 The Lancet Gastroenterology & Hepatology, 'Gender equality in medicine: change is coming', *The Lancet*, 4/12 (2019), 893. doi: 10.1016/S2468-1235(19)30351-6

18 Caroline Criado Perez, *Invisible Women: Exposing Data Bias in a World Designed for Men*, Chatto & Windus: London, 2019.

19 Virginia Eubanks, *Automating Inequality: How High-Tech Tools Profile, Police, and Punish the Poor*, Picador: New York, 2019.

20 Virginia Eubanks, 'We created poverty. Algorithms won't make that go away', *Guardian* (13 May 2018), https://www.theguardian.com/commentisfree/2018/may/13/we-created-poverty-algorithms-wont-make-that-go-away, accessed 13 Dec. 2019.

21 James Vincent, 'Twitter taught Microsoft's AI chatbot to be a racist asshole in less than a day', *The Verge* (24 Mar. 2016), https://www.theverge.com/2016/3/24/11297050/tay-microsoft-chatbot-racist, accessed 11 Jan. 2020.

22 Tom Simonite, 'These Startups Are Building Tools to Keep an Eye on AI', *Wired* (21 Oct. 2019), https://www.wired.com/story/these-startups-are-building-tools-keep-eye-ai/, accessed 13 Jan. 2020.

23 Jeffrey Dastin, 'Amazon scraps secret AI recruiting tool that showed bias against women', *Reuters* (10 Oct. 2018), https://www.reuters.com/article/us-amazon-com-jobs-automation-insight/amazon-scraps-secret-ai-recruiting-tool-that-showed-bias-against-women-idUSKCN1MK08G, accessed 23 Jan. 2020.

24   Tom Simonite, 'When It Comes to Gorillas, Google Photos Remains Blind', *Wired* (11 Jan. 2018), https://www.wired.com/story/when-it-comes-to-gorillas-google-photos-remains-blind, accessed 13 Dec. 2019.

25   Saira Hussain, 'Tell HUD: Algorithms Shouldn't Be an Excuse to Discriminate', *Electronic Frontier Foundation* (18 Oct. 2019), https://www.eff.org/deeplinks/2019/10/tell-hud-algorithms-are-no-excuse-discrimination, accessed 13 Dec. 2019.

26   Mark Townsend, 'Black people "40 times more likely" to be stopped and searched in UK', *Guardian* (4 May 2019), https://www.theguardian.com/law/2019/may/04/stop-and-search-new-row-racial-bias, accessed 11 Jan. 2020.

27   Theodore Schleifer, 'Google CEO Sundar Pichai says AI is more profound than electricity and fire', *Vox* (19 Jan. 2019), https://www.vox.com/2018/1/19/16911180/sundar-pichai-google-fire-electricity-ai, accessed 23 Dec. 2019.

28   The Economist, 'The world's most valuable resource is no longer oil, but data', *The Economist* (6 May 2017), https://www.economist.com/leaders/2017/05/06/the-worlds-most-valuable-resource-is-no-longer-oil-but-data, accessed 13 Dec. 2019.

29   Greg Patro, 'Amazon's Acquisition of Whole Foods is About Two Things: Data and Product, *Forbes* (2 Aug. 2017), https://www.forbes.com/sites/gregpetro/2017/08/02/amazons-acquisition-of-whole-foods-is-about-two-things-data-and-product/, accessed 11 Jan. 2020.

30   J. Sadowski, 'When data is capital: Datafication, accumulation, and extraction', *Big Data & Society*, 6/1 (2019), 1-12. doi: 10.1177/2053951718820549

31   Chloe Watson, 'The key moments from Mark Zuckerberg's testimony to Congress', *Guardian* (11 Apr. 2018), https://www.theguardian.com/technology/2018/apr/11/mark-zuckerbergs-testimony-to-congress-the-key-moments, accessed 11 Jan. 2020.

32   Lynsey Chutel, 'Netflix is finally getting serious about building a library of African movies and shows', *Quartz Africa* (31 May 2018), https://qz.com/africa/1293569/netflix-in-africa-hiring-content-producer-for-africa-turkey-middle-east-more-nollywood-arab-language-shows, accessed 1 Sep. 2019.

33 Ernesto Van der Sar, 'Netflix Dominates Internet Traffic Worldwide, BitTorrent Ranks Fifth', *TorrentFreak* (17 Nov. 2018), https://torrentfreak.com/netflix-dominates-internet-traffic-worldwide-bittorrent-ranks-fifth-181116, accessed 13 Dec. 2019.

34 Rosita Armytage and Markus Bell, 'What the violent "Uber wars" tell us about Zuma's South Africa', *Independent* (16 Sep. 2017), https://www.independent.co.uk/news/world/africa/what-the-violent-uber-wars-tell-us-about-zumas-south-africa-a7948496.html, accessed 13 Dec. 2019.

35 Amy Hawkins, 'Beijing's Big Brother Tech Needs African Faces', *Foreign Policy* (24 Jul. 2018), https://foreignpolicy.com/2018/07/24/beijings-big-brother-tech-needs-african-faces, accessed 13 Dec. 2019.

36 Rodrigue Rwirahira, 'De La Rue set for new generation IDs printing', *The East African* (22 Feb. 2013), https://www.theeastafrican.co.ke/rwanda/News/De-La-Rue-set-for-new-generation-IDs-printing/1433218-1702268-oj4uy8/index.html, accessed 13 Dec. 2019.

37 Kenn Abuya, 'Jumia is Not An African Startup – The Continent is a Means to its End', *Techweez* (15 Apr. 2019), https://techweez.com/2019/04/15/jumia-nyse-not-an-africa-startup/, accessed 23 Dec. 2019.

38 David Pilling, 'Are tech companies Africa's new colonialists?', *Financial Times* (5 Jul. 2019), https://www.ft.com/content/4625d9b8-9c16-11e9-b8ce-8b459ed04726, accessed 9 Jan. 2020.

39 Meredith Broussard, *Artificial Unintelligence: How Computers Misunderstand the World*, MIT Press: Cambridge, Mass., 2018.

40 D. Susser et al., 'Technology, autonomy and manipulation', *Internet Policy Review*, 8/2 (2019). doi: 10.14763/2019.2.1410

41 BBC News, 'Putin: Russian president says liberalism "obsolete"', *BBC* (28 Jun. 2019), https://www.bbc.co.uk/news/world-europe-48795764, accessed 23 Dec. 2019.

42 Michael Hill, 'GDPR is Stifling Innovation, Says Infosec Community', *Infosecurity Magazine* (12 Jul. 2017), https://www.infosecurity-magazine.com/news/gdpr-is-stifling-innovation-says/, accessed 23 Dec. 2019.

43 Anthony Cuthbertson, 'Google Admits Giving Hundreds Of Firms Access To Your Gmail Inbox', *Independent* (21 Sep. 2018), https://www.independent.co.uk/life-style/gadgets-and-tech/news/google-gmail-data-sharing-email-inbox-privacy-scandal-a8548941.html, accessed 11 Jan. 2020.

44 Carole Cadwalladr and Emma Graham-Harrison, 'Revealed: 50 million Facebook profiles harvested for Cambridge Analytica in major data breach', *Guardian* (17 Mar. 2018), https://www.theguardian.com/news/2018/mar/17/cambridge-analytica-facebook-influence-us-election, accessed 23 Dec. 2019.

45 Henry David Thoreau, *Walden*, Enhanced Media Publishing: Los Angeles, 2017, p. 72.

46 C. Apprich et al., *Pattern Discrimination*, University of Minnesota Press: Minneapolis, 2019.

47 Tristan Harris, 'Optimizing for Engagement: Understanding the Use of Persuasive Technology on Internet Platforms', United States Senate Committee on Commerce, Science and Transportation Subcommittee on Communications, Technology, Innovation and the Internet (25 Jun. 2019), http://humanetech.com/wp-content/uploads/2019/06/Testimony-Background-Tristan-Harris_CHT.pdf, accessed 17 Jan. 2019.

48 Statista, 'Most popular social networks worldwide as of October 2019, ranked by number of active users', *Statista* (31 Oct. 2019), https://www.statista.com/statistics/272014/global-social-networks-ranked-by-number-of-users/, accessed 22 Jan. 2020.

49 Nosheen Iqbal, 'Film fans see red over Netflix "targeted" posters for black viewers', *Guardian* (20 Oct. 2018), https://www.theguardian.com/media/2018/oct/20/netflix-film-black-viewers-personalised-marketing-target, accessed 11 Jan. 2020.

50 Kashmir Hill, 'How Target Figured Out A Teen Girl Was Pregnant Before Her Father Did', *Forbes* (16 Feb. 2012), https://www.forbes.com/sites/kashmirhill/2012/02/16/how-target-figured-out-a-teen-girl-was-pregnant-before-her-father-did/, accessed 9 Sep. 2019.

51 Dream McClinton, 'Global attention span is narrowing and trends don't last as long, study reveals', *Guardian* (17 Apr. 2019), https://www.theguardian.com/society/2019/apr/16/got-a-minute-global-attention-span-is-narrowing-study-reveals, accessed 22 Jan. 2020.

52 Paul Mozur, 'A Genocide Incited on Facebook, With Posts From Myanmar's Military', *The New York Times* (15 Oct. 2018), https://www.nytimes.com/2018/10/15/technology/myanmar-facebook-genocide.html, accessed 11 Jan. 2020.

53 C. Miller and R. Coldicutt, *People, Power and Technology: The Tech Workers' View*, Doteveryone (May 2019), https://www.doteveryone.org.uk/wp-content/uploads/2019/04/PeoplePowerTech_Doteveryone_May2019.pdf, accessed 13 Dec. 2019.

54 Frederic Lardinois, 'Google strengthens Chrome's privacy controls', *TechCrunch* (7 May 2019), https://techcrunch.com/2019/05/07/googles-chrome-will-soon-get-new-privacy-features-with-better-cookie-controls-and-anti-fingerprinting-tech/, accessed 11 Jan. 2020.

55 L. Floridi, 'Marketing as Control of Human Interfaces and Its Political Exploitation', *Philosophy & Technology*, 32/3 (2019) 379–388. doi: 10.1007/s13347-019-00374-7

56 National Latina Institute for Reproductive Health, 'Conservatives Argue that Legalized Abortion Encourages Illegal Immigration', National Latina Institute for Reproductive Health (21 Nov. 2006), https://latinainstitute.org/en/content/conservatives-argue-legalized-abortion-encourages-illegal-immigration, accessed 13 Dec. 2019.

57 Zing Tsjeng, 'Brazil's New President Once Told a Politician She Was Too Ugly to Rape', *Vice* (29 Oct. 2018), https://www.vice.com/en_us/article/j53wx8/jair-bolsonaro-elected-president-brazil, accessed 11 Jan. 2020.

58 Reuters, 'Rodrigo Duterte jokes to soldiers that they can rape women with impunity', *Guardian* (27 May 2017), https://www.theguardian.com/world/2017/may/27/rodrigo-duterte-jokes-to-soldiers-that-they-can-women-with-impunity, accessed 11 Jan. 2020.

59 Hannah Ellis-Petersen, 'Philippines: Rodrigo Duterte orders soldiers to shoot female rebels "in the vagina"', *Guardian* (13 Feb. 2018), https://www.theguardian.com/world/2018/feb/13/philippines-rodrigo-duterte-orders-soldiers-to-shoot-female-rebels-in-the-vagina, accessed 11 Jan. 2020.

60 Tom Embury-Dennis, 'Alabama sued over law which bans abortion even in cases of rape and incest', *Independent* (24

May 2019), https://www.independent.co.uk/news/world/americas/us-politics/alabama-abortion-ban-aclu-lawsuit-pro-life-planned-parenthood-family-planning-a8929246.html, accessed 11 Jan. 2020.

61   Madelyn Webb and Natalie Martinez, 'Study: Right-wing sources dominate abortion-related news on Facebook', *Media Matters for America* (28 May 2019), https://www.mediamatters.org/facebook/study-right-wing-sources-dominate-abortion-related-news-facebook, accessed 13 Dec. 2019.

62   BBC News, 'Vote Leave's targeted Brexit ads released by Facebook', *BBC* (26 Jul. 2018), https://www.bbc.co.uk/news/uk-politics-44966969, accessed 11 Jan. 2020.

63   Carole Cadwalladr, 'Fresh Cambridge Analytica leak "shows global manipulation is out of control"', *Guardian* (4 Jan. 2020), https://www.theguardian.com/uk-news/2020/jan/04/cambridge-analytica-data-leak-global-election-manipulation, accessed 9 Jan. 2020.

64   J. Sadowski, 'When data is capital: Datafication, accumulation and extraction', *Big Data & Society*, 6/1 (2019), 1–12. doi: 10.1177/2053951718820549

65   Mary Hui, 'Why Hong Kong's protesters were afraid to use their metro cards', *Quartz* (13 Jun. 2019), https://qz.com/1642441/extradition-law-why-hong-kong-protesters-didnt-use-own-metro-cards/, accessed 9 Jan. 2020.

66   Zeynep Tufekci, 'How social media took us from Tahrir Square to Donald Trump', *MIT Technology Review* (14 Aug. 2018), https://www.technologyreview.com/s/611806/how-social-media-took-us-from-tahrir-square-to-donald-trump/, accessed 23 Dec. 2019.

67   John Naughton, '"The goal is to automate us": welcome to the age of surveillance capitalism', *Guardian* (20 Jan. 2019), https://www.theguardian.com/technology/2019/jan/20/shoshana-zuboff-age-of-surveillance-capitalism-google-facebook, accessed 13 Dec. 2019.

68   Leo Kelion, 'Amazon heads off facial recognition rebellion', *BBC* (22 May 2019), https://www.bbc.co.uk/news/technology-48339142, accessed 13 Dec. 2019.

69   An Amazon Employee, 'I'm an Amazon Employee. My Company Shouldn't Sell Facial Recognition Tech to Police', *Medium*

(16 Oct. 2018), https://medium.com/@amazon_employee/im-an-amazon-employee-my-company-shouldn-t-sell-facial-recognition-tech-to-police-36b5fde934ac, accessed 23 Dec. 2019.

70 Dave Lee, 'San Francisco is first US city to ban facial recognition', *BBC* (15 May 2019), https://www.bbc.co.uk/news/technology-48276660, accessed 13 Nov. 2019.

71 Jacqueline Alemany, 'White House considers new project seeking links between mental health and violent behavior', *The Washington Post* (22 Aug. 2019), https://www.washingtonpost.com/politics/2019/08/22/white-house-considers-new-project-seeking-links-between-mental-health-violent-behavior/, accessed 8 Sep. 2019.

72 Hilary Brueck and Shana Lebowitz, 'The men behind the US's deadliest mass shootings have domestic violence – not mental illness – in common', *Business Insider* (5 Aug. 2019), https://www.businessinsider.com/deadliest-mass-shootings-almost-all-have-domestic-violence-connection-2017-11?r=US&IR=T, accessed 22 Jan. 2020.

73 Tom Slee, 'The incompatible incentives of private sector AI', Tom Slee Blog (Mar. 2019), https://tomslee.github.io/publication/oup_private_sector_ai/, accessed 22 Jan. 2020.

74 Virginia Eubanks, *Automating Inequality: How High-Tech Tools Profile, Police and Punish the Poor*, St Martin's Press: New York, 2018.

75 Cathy O'Neil, *Weapons of Math Destruction: How Big Data Increases Inequality and Threatens Democracy*, Crown: New York, 2016.

76 Noam Scheiber, 'How Uber Uses Psychological Tricks to Push Its Drivers' Buttons', *New York Times* (2 Apr. 2017), https://www.nytimes.com/interactive/2017/04/02/technology/uber-drivers-psychological-tricks.html, accessed 8 Sep. 2019.

77 Dina Gerdeman, 'The Airbnb Effect: Cheaper Rooms for Travelers, Less Revenue for Hotels', *Forbes* (27 Feb. 2018), https://www.forbes.com/sites/hbsworkingknowledge/2018/02/27/the-airbnb-effect-cheaper-rooms-for-travelers-less-revenue-for-hotels/#581fe36d672f, accessed 22 Jan. 2020.

78 Kevin Kelleher, 'Facebook Content Moderators Take Home Minimum Wage, Anxiety, and Trauma, Report Says', *Fortune* (25 Feb. 2019), https://fortune.com/2019/02/25/facebook-

content-moderators-trauma-anxiety-disturbing-content/, accessed 11 Jan. 2020.

79   S. T. Roberts, 'Digital Refuse: Canadian Garbage, commercial content moderation and the global circulation of social media's waste', *Journal of Mobile Media*, 10/1 (2016), 1–18, http://wi.mobilities.ca/digitalrefuse/, accessed 17 Jan. 2020.

80   Alan Winfield, 'Energy and Exploitation: AIs dirty secrets', *Alan Winfield's Web Log* (28 Jun. 2019), https://alanwinfield.blogspot.com/2019/06/energy-and-exploitation-ais-dirty.html, accessed 11 Jan. 2019.

81   Julia Carrie Wong, '"A white-collar sweatshop": Google Assistant contractors allege wage theft', *Guardian* (25 Jun. 2019), https://www.theguardian.com/technology/2019/may/28/a-white-collar-sweatshop-google-assistant-contractors-allege-wage-theft, accessed 23 Dec. 2019.

82   Mary L. Gray and Siddharth Suri, *Ghost Work: How to Stop Silicon Valley from Building a New Global Underclass*, Houghton Mifflin Harcourt: Boston, 2019.

83   University of Wisconsin Data Science, 'How Much Is a Data Scientist's Salary?', *University of Wisconsin Data Science* (15 Sep. 2017), https://datasciencedegree.wisconsin.edu/data-science/data-scientist-salary/, accessed 23 Dec. 2019.

84   James Vincent, 'Google employee who helped lead protests leaves company', *The Verge* (16 Jul. 2019), https://www.theverge.com/2019/7/16/20695964/google-protest-leader-meredith-whittaker-leaves-company, accessed 13 Dec. 2019.

85   Marisa Franco, 'Tech workers must unite to defeat America's deportation machine', *Guardian* (26 Jul. 2018), https://www.theguardian.com/commentisfree/2018/jul/26/tech-workers-us-immigration-protests-activism, accessed 9 Sep. 2019.

86   Maya Kosoff, 'Amazon Workers to Jeff Bezos: Stop Weaponizing Our Tech', *Vanity Fair* (22 Jun. 2018), https://www.vanityfair.com/news/2018/06/amazon-workers-to-jeff-bezos-stop-weaponizing-our-tech, accessed 16 Jan. 2020.

87   Jack Shenker, *Now We Have Your Attention: The New Politics of the People*, The Bodley Head: London, 2019.

88   Masego Madzwamuse, 'Artificial Intelligence and Women's Rights', *TEDx Talks* (29 Nov. 2017), https://m.youtube.com/watch?v=Phehwwm1ULI, accessed 8 Sep. 2019.

89 Eurostat, 'Gender Pay Gap statistics' *Eurostat* (5 Mar. 2019), https://ec.europa.eu/eurostat/statistics-explained/index.php/Gender_pay_gap_statistics, accessed 23 Dec. 2019.

90 Clare McDonald, 'Less than a quarter of AI professionals are women', *ComputerWeekly* (21 Dec. 2018), https://www.computerweekly.com/news/252454841/Less-than-a-quarter-of-AI-professionals-are-women, accessed 23 Dec. 2019.

91 Marc Tracy and Tiffany Hsu, 'Director of M.I.T.'s Media Lab Resigns After Taking Money From Jeffrey Epstein', *New York Times* (7 Sep. 2019), https://www.nytimes.com/2019/09/07/business/mit-media-lab-jeffrey-epstein-joichi-ito.html, accessed 22 Aug. 2019.

92 Meredith Broussard, *Artificial Unintelligence: How Computers Misunderstand the World*, MIT Press: Cambridge, Mass., 2018.

93 Cory Booker, 'Booker, Wyden, Clarke Introduce Bill Requiring Companies To Target Bias in Corporate Algorithms', *Cory Booker* (10 Apr. 2019), https://www.booker.senate.gov/?p=press_release&id=903, accessed 22 Jan. 2020.

94 Kelsey D. Atherton, 'Are Killer Robots the Future of War? Parsing the Facts on Autonomous Weapons', *New York Times* (15 Nov. 2018), https://www.nytimes.com/2018/11/15/magazine/autonomous-robots-weapons.html, accessed 23 Dec. 2019.

95 David Smith, 'Pentagon seeks "ethicist" to oversee military artificial intelligence', *Guardian* (7 Sep. 2019), https://www.theguardian.com/us-news/2019/sep/07/pentagon-military-artificial-intelligence-ethicist, accessed 13 Dec. 2019.

96 Wikipedia, 'Sophia (robot)', *Wikipedia* (22 Jan. 2020), https://en.wikipedia.org/wiki/Sophia_(robot), accessed 25 Jan. 2020.

97 Megan Specia, 'Saudi Arabia Granted Women the Right to Drive. A Year on, It's Still Complicated.', *New York Times* (24 Jun. 2019), https://www.nytimes.com/2019/06/24/world/middleeast/saudi-driving-ban-anniversary.html, accessed 8 Sep. 2019.

98 Rodrigo Ochigame, 'The Invention of "Ethical AI": How Big Tech Manipulates Academia to Avoid Regulation', *The Intercept* (20 Dec. 2019), https://theintercept.com/2019/12/20/mit-ethical-ai-artificial-intelligence/, accessed 12 Jan. 2020.

99 Y. Shoham et al., ' The AI Index 2018 Annual Report', AI Index Steering Committee, Human-Centred AI Initiative,

Stanford University (Dec. 2018), https://cdn.aiindex.org/2018/AI%20Index%202018%20Annual%20Report.pdf, accessed 23 Dec. 2019.

100 A. Jobin, M. Ienca, E. Vayena, 'Artificial Intelligence: the global landscape of ethics guidelines', *Health Ethics & Policy Lab* (2019), https://arxiv.org/pdf/1906.11668.pdf, accessed 23 Dec. 2019.

101 Agence France-Presse, 'More than 20 ambassadors condemn China's treatment of Uighurs in Xinjiang', *The Guardian* (11 Jul. 2019), https://www.theguardian.com/world/2019/jul/11/more-than-20-ambassadors-condemn-chinas-treatment-of-uighurs-in-xinjiang, accessed 16 Jan. 2020.

102 Ryan Gallagher, 'How U.S. Tech Giants Are Helping to Build China's Surveillance State', *The Intercept* (11 Jul. 2019), https://theintercept.com/2019/07/11/china-surveillance-google-ibm-semptian, accessed 13 Dec. 2019.

103 James Vincent, 'Putin says the nation that leads in AI "will be the ruler of the world"', *The Verge* (4 Sep. 2017), https://www.theverge.com/2017/9/4/16251226/russia-ai-putin-rule-the-world, accessed 12 Sep. 2019.

104 Paul Ratner, 'Putin Weighs in on Artificial Intelligence and Elon Musk Is Alarmed', *Big Think* (24 Sep. 2017), https://bigthink.com/paul-ratner/putin-weighs-in-on-artificial-intelligence-and-elon-musk-is-alarmed, accessed 13 Dec. 2019.

105 Oliver Burkeman, 'Dirty Secrets: why is there still a housework gender gap?', *Guardian* (17 Feb. 2018), https://www.theguardian.com/inequality/2018/feb/17/dirty-secret-why-housework-gender-gap, accessed 13 Dec. 2019.

106 Haroon Siddique, 'NHS teams up with Amazon to bring Alexa to patients', *Guardian* (10 Jul. 2019), https://www.theguardian.com/society/2019/jul/10/nhs-teams-up-with-amazon-to-bring-alexa-to-patients, accessed 23 Dec. 2019.

107 World Health Organization, 'Violence against women: Definition and scope of the problem', *World Health Organization* (Jul. 1997), https://www.who.int/gender/violence/v4.pdf, accessed 23 Dec. 2019.

108 Alina Tugend, 'Exposing the Bias Embedded in Tech', *New York Times* (17 Jun. 2019), https://www.nytimes.com/2019/06/17/

business/artificial-intelligence-bias-tech.html, accessed 12 Dec. 2019.

109 Casey Newton, 'Brain-computer interfaces are developing faster than the policy debate around them', *The Verge* (31 Jul. 2019), https://www.theverge.com/interface/2019/7/31/20747916/facebook-brain-computer-interface-policy-neuralink, accessed 9 Jan. 2020.

110 Dani Deahl, 'The EU plans to test an AI lie detector at border points', *The Verge* (31 Oct. 2018), https://www.theverge.com/2018/10/31/18049906/eu-artificial-intelligence-ai-lie-detector-border-points-immigration, accessed 8 Sep. 2019.

111 Daniel Boffey, 'EU border "lie detector" system criticised as pseudoscience', *Guardian* (2 Nov. 2018), https://www.theguardian.com/world/2018/nov/02/eu-border-lie-detection-system-criticised-as-pseudoscience, accessed 13 Dec. 2019; see also, Homo Digitalis, 'Greece: Clarifications sought on human rights impacts of iBorderCtrl', *European Digital Rights* (21 Nov. 2018) https://edri.org/greece-clarifications-sought-on-human-rights-impacts-of-iborderctrl, accessed 13 Dec. 2019.

112 Massachusetts Institute of Technology, '6.904 Ethics for Engineers', *Massachusetts Institute of Technology*, https://www.eecs.mit.edu/academics-admissions/academic-information/subject-updates-ft-2015/6904, accessed 9 Nov. 2019.

113 C. P. Limpangog, 'Matrix of Domination' in N. Naples et al. (eds.), *The Wiley Blackwell Encyclopedia of Gender and Sexuality Studies*, Wiley & Sons: New Jersey, 2016.

114 L. Floridi, 'Translating Principles into Practices of Digital Ethics: Five Risks of Being Unethical', *Philosophy & Technology* 32/2 (2019), 185–93. doi: 10.1007/s13347-019-00354-x.

115 Sonia Elks, 'Hey Siri, you're sexist, finds UN report on gendered technology', *World Economic Forum* (31 May 2019), https://www.weforum.org/agenda/2019/05/hey-siri-youre-sexist-finds-u-n-report-on-gendered-technology/, accessed 13 Dec. 2019.

116 Laura Bates, 'The Trouble With Sex Robots', *New York Times* (17 Jul. 2017), https://www.nytimes.com/2017/07/17/opinion/sex-robots-consent.html, accessed 13 Dec. 2019.

117 Jack Callil, 'The Surprisingly Sensitive World of Men who Own Sex Dolls', *Vice* (16 Feb. 2015), https://www.vice.com/

en_us/article/dpwnwy/the-surprisingly-sensitive-world-of-men-who-own-sex-dolls, accessed 8 Sep. 2019.

118 Rob Waugh, 'Men at tech fair molest £3,000 sex robot so much it's left broken and "heavily soiled"', *Metro* (27 Sep. 2017), https://metro.co.uk/2017/09/27/men-at-tech-fair-molest-3000-sex-robot-so-much-its-left-broken-and-heavily-soiled-6960778/?ito=cbshare, accessed 8 Sep. 2019.

119 Jenny Kleeman, 'The race to build the world's first sex robot', *Guardian* (27 Apr. 2017), https://www.theguardian.com/technology/2017/apr/27/race-to-build-world-first-sex-robot, accessed 13 Dec. 2019.

120 Tom Dart, '"Keep robot brothels out of Houston": sex doll company faces pushback', *Guardian* (2 Oct. 2018), https://www.theguardian.com/us-news/2018/oct/01/houston-robot-brothel-kinky-s-dolls-sex-trafficking, accessed 13 Dec. 2019.

121 Lin Taylor, 'Sex robots: perverted or practical in fight against sex trafficking?' *Reuters* (20 Jul. 2017), https://www.reuters.com/article/us-science-robots-sextrafficking/sex-robots-perverted-or-practical-in-fight-against-sex-trafficking-idUSKBN1A50HD, accessed 22 Jan. 2020.

122 Shirin Ghaffary, 'It's been a year since 20,000 Google employees walked off the job. And they're madder than ever', *Vox* (1 Nov. 2019), https://www.vox.com/platform/amp/recode/2019/11/1/20942234/google-walkout-one-year-anniversary-unionization-organizing-tech-activism-we-wont-built-it, accessed 13 Dec. 2019.

123 Shannon Liao, 'Google confirms it agreed to pay $135 million to two execs accused of sexual harassment', *The Verge* (11 Mar. 2019), https://www.theverge.com/2019/3/11/18260712/google-amit-singhal-andy-rubin-payout-lawsuit-accused-sexual-harassment, accessed 8 Sep. 2019.

124 L. Winner, 'Do Artifacts Have Politics?' *Daedalus*, 109/1 (1980), 121–36, http://www.jstor.org/stable/20024652, accessed 13 Dec. 2019.

125 Global Climate Change, 'Scientific Consensus: Earth's Climate is Warming', *Global Climate Change* (28 Jan. 2020), https://climate.nasa.gov/scientific-consensus/, accessed 9 Jan. 2020.

ACKNOWLEDGEMENTS

This book would not have been possible without the support, advice and generosity of so many people.

My colleagues in the Women Leading in AI Network and our allies for the collective thinking, the sharing of knowledge, the exchange of ideas. A special thanks to Samara Banno, Allison Gardner, Rebecca Geah, Emma Gibson, Ben Gilburt, Andrew Pakes, Reema Patel, Trish Shaw, Sanya Sheikh and Liz Stocks. May the Network continue go from strength to strength as it is very much needed.

Megan Corton-Scott for all the brainstorming at the early stages of the book. Susie Gilbert for the spirited nudges. Gianni Ciolli for the technical advice. Annajoy David for all the hours of passionate political discussions.

My husband James who believes in me, and my parents Alberto and Lina who taught me and many others.

Rachel Adams, Seyi Akiwowo, Maria Luciana Axente, Nina Barakzai, Laura Bates, Abeba Birhane, Meredith Broussard, Joanna Bryson, Carole Cadwalladr, Ann Cavoukian, Rumman Chowdhury, Rachel Coldicutt, Kate Crawford, Caroline Criado-Perez, Sue Daley, Mia Dand, Elizabeth Denham, Virginia Dignum, Kay Firth-Butterfield, Tabitha Goldstaub, Wendy Hall, Gry Hasselbach, Carly Kind, Nora Ni Loideain, Madhumita Murgia, Gina Neff, Mutale Nkonde, Safiya Noble, Cathy O'Neil, Imogen Parker, Sarah Porter, Maria Rosaria Taddeo, Francesca Rossi, Zeynep Tufekci, Margrethe Vestager, Meredith Whittaker and all the other women trailblazers, I thank you.

ABOUT THE AUTHOR

IVANA BARTOLETTI is a privacy and ethics consultant, and supports businesses in their privacy by design programmes, especially in relation to Artificial Intelligence and blockchain technology. Her interests include AI, data ethics and feminism. She co-founded the Women Leading in AI Network, a lobby group that empowers women to shape the norms of AI, and is the Chair of the Fabian Society. Ivana was named Woman of the Year 2019 in the Cyber Security Awards. She lives in London.

THE

INDIGO

PRESS

Sign up for our newsletter and receive exclusive updates, including extracts, podcasts, event notifications, competitions and more.

www.theindigopress.com/newsletter

Follow The Indigo Press:

@PressIndigoThe
@TheIndigoPress
@TheIndigoPress